ID621863

KIANTONE

CHAUTAUQUA COUNTY'S
MYSTICAL VALLEY

Deborah K. Cronin

Bloomington, IN Milton Keynes, UK

authorHOUSE

AuthorHouse™
1663 Liberty Drive, Suite 200
Bloomington, IN 47403
www.authorhouse.com
Phone: 1-800-839-8640

AuthorHouse™ UK Ltd.
500 Avebury Boulevard
Central Milton Keynes, MK9 2BE
www.authorhouse.co.uk
Phone: 08001974150

© 2006 Deborah K. Cronin. All rights reserved.

No part of this book may be reproduced, stored in a retrieval system, or transmitted by any means without the written permission of the author.

First published by AuthorHouse 5/11/2006

ISBN: 1-4259-3465-X (e)
ISBN: 1-4259-3475-7 (sc)

Library of Congress Control Number: 2006903687

Printed in the United States of America
Bloomington, Indiana

This book is printed on acid-free paper.

Speak of me as I am, nothing extenuate
nor set down in malice.

- **Othello**, as quoted by Oliver
F. Chase and Emma Hardinge
when writing about Kiantone's
Harmonia Community

TABLE OF CONTENTS

NOTE ABOUT SOURCES

This book could not have been written without the diligent work of many different people over a period exceeding two hundred years. Some of the resources they produced were helpful, while others were cryptic, confusing, or simply contained historical errors.

As I poured over the resources, it became obvious that I needed to share with my readers which resources proved most helpful in writing this book. I established evaluation criteria for organizing the material into three groups: *primary, secondary,* and *tertiary documents.*

Primary documents, by my definition, were mostly historical records created by persons who actually experienced Kiantone's history in the making. These included letters and reports, many of which are contained in the *Sheldon Papers,* located in the *Darlington Memorial Collection* at the *University of Pittsburgh.* I also made extensive use of John Murray Spear's autobiographical pamphlet, *Twenty Years on the Wing: Brief Narrative of My Travels and Labors as a Missionary Sent Forth and Sustained by the Association of Beneficents in the Spirit Land.* In a few cases, transcriptions of séances were used, but only sparingly and usually when information contained in them directly related to actions and initiatives taken by those who received them. Much of the lofty, utopian concepts that Spear and his group embraced were acquired through séances. In this book I have not dwelled on these concepts, but they were collected in a work titled, *The Educator,* which may be found in various reserve libraries and literary collections.

Also included in the primary resource category were newspaper accounts from the 1850s and eyewitness accounts recorded by persons who were not directly part of Kiantone's *Harmonia* community, but closely observed its activities. For example, *Modern American Spiritualism: A Twenty Years' Record of the Communion Between Earth and the World of Spirits,* by Emma Hardinge, proved helpful. Spear and Hardinge were contemporaries and moved in similar Spiritualist circles. Mrs. Hardinge, a Spiritualist medium, was an early prolific chronicler of *Spiritualism* in the United States. Her work shows intense attention to research and detail, although her writing style is sometimes both quirky and harsh.

Although they are not primary documents in the strict sense of the term, I also made use of Gregory R. Yaw's college honors paper, *An American Worldview: The Cosmos and Society in a Radical Worldview on the Eve of the Civil War,* and Russell Duino's masters thesis, *The Domain at Spiritual Springs: A Short History of the Kiantone Harmonia, Together with a Calendar of the Sheldon Papers from the Collection of Ernest C. Miller, Warren, Pennsylvania.* It should be noted that Russell Duino also compiled an index for the *Sheldon Papers* that is located with the *Sheldon Papers* at the Darlington Memorial Library. Both of these men worked meticulously with the *Sheldon Papers* under the supervision of their academic professors. However, as Yaw rightly pointed out in his paper, Duino's numbering contains two slight errors. All my references to the *Sheldon Papers* correspond to the numbering found in Duino's calendar, which is an incredibly helpful tool in unraveling the Harmonia saga. As I researched my book and spoke with these helpful gentlemen, I became ever more confident of the validity of their material. Due to a vision impairment, I also became ever more reliant on their work because of the current faded and fragile condition of the *Sheldon Papers.*

Finally, I also included John L. Young's essay, *Free Love in the 1800s: The Kiantone Harmonia,* among the primary documents. Mr. Young prepared his paper in close conversation with Gregory Yaw and with dedicated attention to details as found in the *Sheldon Papers.*

Secondary documents were those articles and books written by persons who did not directly experience the events described. These included histories from the mid to late 1800s and early 1900s. These histories covered a wide range of topics related to Kiantone. Pertaining to the Harmonia community, some were kindly toward the Spiritualist movement and others were unsympathetic. Suffice it to say that some writers recorded history and others wrote a history biased by their own subjective feelings and attitudes. Also included in the secondary documents category were newspaper articles from the 20th Century. These were often written with a negative bias against the Harmonia community. Occasional articles in tourist and local interest publications were also in this group.

Tertiary documents were those books, diagrams, and maps I used that were related to the general themes, ideas, and events included in this book. These ranged from Mark Twain's *Life on the Mississippi* to William Hoover's book, *Kinzua: from Cornplanter to the Corps.* This category also included *Internet* websites. These proved useful in learning about the various historical characters involved, or believed to be involved, in different aspects of Kiantone's history. History is told, of course, in the eye of the beholder, or in the 21st Century, we might say in the data of the webmaster. However, I was impressed and greatly aided by the Internet resources used in this project. I was also very aware that, because of the gigantic amount of material readily available today on the Internet, I was able to connect dots in the story that eluded researches and writers in the past. For this, I am grateful.

Scattered throughout this book the reader will find maps showing locations of various towns, cities, and geographical features. I consider myself to be the *Grandma Moses* of cartography. Those wishing more sophisticated maps can find them on the Internet and at your local library.

One of my main goals in writing this book was to filter through the enormous amount of written material available on this subject. It was my clear intent to leave a navigable roadmap through the resources, documents, and literature of this story. The reader will note that I included many endnotes using my own endnote style that combines the classical endnote style with the scientific notation style. In this manner, quotations should be simple to connect to the resources from whence they came. According to *public domain* copyright laws, most of these endnotes would not have been necessary but I provided them to assist further research projects. In addition, *italics* were used throughout the book to designate, in most cases, first use of names, places, and ideas. The reader will find, but I hope not be bothered, by the numerous italics and endnotes. I am in hopes that more historians, both professional and amateur, will use them as road signs for their own enjoyable trip through the history of one of America's most interesting small rural communities.

One last word remains to be said about the creation of this book. It was the most fun I have ever had writing any piece of literature. The various people that lived in and passed through Kiantone during the late 1700s and early to mid-1800s ranged from unique to unexceptional, from quixotic to realistic, as well as often being both amusing and amazing! The more I worked on this book, the more I liked all the people I read about and the more I wanted to share their story with others.

Can anything good come out of Kiantone? I positively, not negatively, believe that it can!

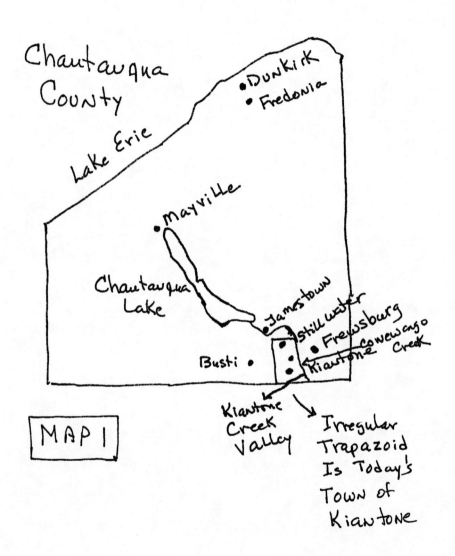

Chautauqua County

• Dunkirk
• Fredonia

Lake Erie

• Mayville

Chautauqua Lake

Jamestown
• Stillwater
• Frewsburg
Kiantone • Cowewago Creek

Busti •

Kiantone Creek Valley

Irregular Trapazoid Is Today's Town of Kiantone

MAP 1

INTRODUCTION

Thunder in the Valley

I remember the first time I heard thunder in the *Kiantone Valley*. Initially, I had no idea what it was. It did not sound like thunder. As I listened more closely, I thought that someone nearby was using dynamite because the sound had an explosive quality. It echoed and shook down the steep sides of the valley. Finally, I realized it must be thunder, and so I hurried back to my summer house to escape the impending storm. That was in 1997.

I first heard of the Kiantone area when I was a child. My parents had purchased property in Kiantone (Map 1) several years before I was born. The site, located in *Chautauqua County* on the hill between *Stillwater Creek* and the *Pennsylvania* and *New York* state line, had a beautiful view of the *Conewango Creek Valley*. My father's plan was to dig out and construct a basement foundation for the house, in which my parents and toddler-age sister would live in until he was able to complete the one-story ranch house they envisioned.

But this dream was not to be. My father's health had been weakened by malaria during World War II when he was stationed for a time in Guatemala. Throughout his life a heavy cold or the flu would somehow trigger the lingering malaria in his system. He was not strong enough to work all day at *Blackstone Corporation* where he helped make automobile heater units, and then work on the house evenings and weekends.

So the dream was revised. My parents sold the lot in Kiantone and bought a small house in Ashville that had been built by my maternal great-grandfather, George Butts. This was the same house where my mother had been raised by her grandparents until she was thirteen. In time, my parents turned this modest house into a comfortable and tidy small home.

Still, even though she was sympathetic to my father's health, my mother always lamented their not being able to build the home in Kiantone. So I was not surprised many years later, when Mother, by then a widow after a long marriage to my father, suggested we purchase a small travel trailer and place it for a summer home at a campground located in the Kiantone Valley. I surprised her by instead purchasing a nice mobile home, a *park model* as they call it. Our friend, the late Gordon Anderson, a retired shop teacher and master carpenter, built a lovely deck and easily accessible stairs to surround the park model. We were happy with this summer home, available to us for the best six months of each year.

We had not been at the campground very long before our neighbors discovered that I am an ordained clergywoman. Learning that, they told us that the Kiantone Valley had once been used for camp meetings. This, I understood them to say, was back in the days of the early 1800s when evangelical Protestant Christians held lively outdoor worship services in rustic settings.

It made sense to me. We were located on the south side of the *Kiantone Creek* beside a round open area with many tall sycamore trees. In my mind's eye I could imagine rough hewn log benches being built around a timbered altar. I could see wagons full of those hardy early settlers coming down the steep lane that led to the grove. No doubt they would enjoy the creek-side camp meeting week, a time for both *getting saved* and fellowship with their friends and neighbors.

While at our summer place in Kiantone, I wrote most of *Holy Ground: Celtic Christian Spirituality.* The book was an exploration of my spiritual roots in Ireland and Scotland. After extended visits to both countries, the Kiantone Valley seemed like an equally impressive natural spot for reflection. Often I would ruminate about having such a beautiful outdoor setting in which to write that book since it was a place, as our friends had told us, that also had a history of Christian fervor and excitement.

And, then, about three months before we left Western New York and moved to Indiana, one of our camp neighbors told us that the site had not been used for camp meetings at all. When we inquired about how it had been used, he rather sheepishly told us that in the mid-1800s it had been a nudist colony.

Well, we laughed to ourselves, thinking that the joke had truly been on us! Here we had spent wonderful springs, summers, and autumns in this place, thinking it had this fascinating Christian spiritual history, only to learn that folks had frolicked there *sans* clothing.

Just a week or so before leaving, we got a bit closer to the truth. A second friend told us that it was never used as a nudist colony and, to my knowledge now, it was not then nor ever used in that manner. This friend supplied us with a photocopy of an article written by *William S. Bailey* in 1924 for the Jamestown *University Club.* The club actually held a meeting at the *Kiantone Springs* located in the valley. At that meeting Mr. Bailey presented his paper. Reading the article we were astonished to learn that the Kiantone Valley had been the site of a Spiritualist colony in the 1850s.

Spiritualism, according to the *Merriam-Webster Online Diction-ary,* is *belief that spirits of the dead communicate with the living usually through a medium.* It is not encouraged nor embraced by orthodox Christianity. So, for a Christian clergywoman and her devout mother, it was a bit disconcerting to learn that we had fallen in love with a place that once entertained what seemed to us as very strange activities. But, we were philosophical about the whole experience, deciding, in the end, that we had loved the time we spent in the little valley by the creek, and so we would not take its past too seriously. I tucked the historical article into my tickler file for future writing projects and promptly forgot about it.

Several summers later, I decided to spend my vacation visiting friends in Chautauqua County. My mother had passed away in May after a lengthy illness at a nursing home in Indiana. While tending to her, I had not returned to Chautauqua County, the place we call *home*, even though we had lived in various states. The vacation afforded me the opportunity to spend time with good friends and entertain myself with my favorite hobby, American History, particularly from the mid-1800s.

One person's blessing is another person's bane. So, I understand that one might not want to spend a vacation this way. But on my vacation, I devoted several happy and contented days to researching the story of the Kiantone Spiritualist community. Day after day, I sat in the *Smith Memorial Library* at *Chautauqua Institution*, as well as the *Fenton History Center – Museum and Library*, and the *Prendergast Library* in Jamestown, NY, studying essays, newspaper articles, and pages from early Chautauqua County history books.

Back home in Indiana, I continued to read related articles, books, and Internet sites, gleaning whatever I could about this 19th Century Spiritualist experiment. It did not take me long to realize that this would be the topic of my next book. This story had me in its clutches. This was not because I was persuaded to become a Spiritualist. Rather, I was captivated by how the remarkable histories of the Kiantone settlement, the City of Jamestown and Chautauqua County, as well as Western New York and Pennsylvania, and even New England, swirled among Kiantone's Spiritualist events and characters. And, much to my surprise and delight, there was even an Indiana connection to the saga. The folks in Indiana call themselves *Hoosiers*, and as a Hoosier wannabe, that sealed the deal!

Much of the recorded history of Kiantone's Spiritualist community is taken from secondary sources, articles written in the late 1800s and early 1900s. In addition, there is an excellent collection of original, also called primary, documents that belonged to the community's chief financial supporter, Thaddeus S. Sheldon, an 18th Century businessman who lived in Randolph, New York. These are housed at the University of Pittsburgh in the Darlington Memorial Collection. Perhaps most fascinating among the primary documents are the writings of John Murray Spear, the community's spiritual leader.

As I reviewed this material, something inside me said it was time to pull together the various threads of this story and give it a renewed telling in the language of my own time. To my great surprise, I found that in the midst of this work some of the threads of my own story were pulled together as well. That is why I have written this book in the grammatical first person. I love the story of the people of Kiantone, and I love how they have helped me better understand the culture and happenings of the 1800s. In researching and writing the book I was also truly blessed by the various historians, both professional and amateur and both living and dead, that I encountered along the way. I also found the Kiantone story, with its many diverse characters and locations, to be just good old-fashion, entertaining fun!

But, something stronger tugged on me whenever I reviewed my notes about *Harmonia*, one of the names by which this Spiritualist community was called. The secondary articles I read were mostly critical and scathing of Harmonia's key players and their intentions. This was understandable given the time in which the articles were written. However, the harsh criticism bothered me, often at a deep gut level. Eventually, I was able to identify the reasons for my irritation.

First, as I peeled back the layers of history present in Kiantone, I was impressed by how the beauty and unique nature of the area had drawn a variety of equally unique peoples. What, I wondered, was the purpose for this place, and how did so many people come to find it to be a place where the unusual was experienced?

Second, my reflections brought me to this observation: today we live in a time of great mistrust among many religious people. This has been played out graphically, for example, in the way some *Christians* and *Jews* view and act towards the *Muslim* faith, countries, and people. We see this in the acts of hatred directed toward Muslims since the terrorism of *9/11*. *Radical Muslims* have likewise been harsh critics of other religions and some have committed frightening terrorist acts in the name of God.

And yet, this is America. In this country, one of our most beloved values is that of *Amendment I* of *The Bill of Rights*, specifically the first two clauses: *Congress shall make no law respecting the establishment of religion, or prohibiting the free exercise thereof…*

I am a Christian; I believe that Christianity is God's best revelation of God's divinity. I trust the promises and embrace the hope of the Christian Trinity. I expect to die a Christian. And, as you will see in this book, I personally do not believe that Christianity, even in its more moderate expressions, can embrace Spiritualism. Still, there is a *paradox* in my beliefs. This is because I am both a Christian and an American. I am compelled, therefore, to be willing to both live and, if need be, die for all American freedoms, including the right to worship and believe as one chooses.

And, so, I have written this book, first, because I am a lover of American history, and second, because the story of Kiantone's many peoples, including the Seneca and early pioneers, deserve a fresh, appreciative 21st Century re-telling. Third, as to Kiantone's Spiritualist community, I hope I can faithfully and with integrity tell the story of a group of American citizens who were Spiritualists and so much more. These people boldly chose a different path. That path took them to the beautiful Kiantone Valley in Chautauqua County, to great rivers and cities of our nation, and to ideas and actions that may seem to others simultaneously both mystical and foolish. They lived in a time when clashing principles and the threat of war on American soil thundered across the nation. Yet, somehow, in the midst of the impending storm, they found a way to make sense of it all, at least from their perspective. They were spiritual thinkers, compassionate servants, and creative doers. Their story deserves a thunderous re-telling. I hope I can accomplish that task.

CHAPTER 1

THE VALLEY

Unique and Hidden

The people who come to the Kiantone Valley today, I am sure, do not come primarily for its mystical environment. For them, it is a place for recreation and relaxation. In the beginning of the 21st Century, this valley contains a large three-season campground, several summer homes, and a few year-round homes. The valley, which abuts the New York and Pennsylvania state line, is tucked into the south-southeast area of the *Town of Kiantone* (Map 1). It is roughly three-quarters of a mile long by one-quarter wide and has a sharply rising northwest side that rises to 1,350 feet and a similar southeast side that rises to an altitude of 1,300 feet. The overall topography of the Town of Kiantone is undulating in the east and hilly in the west. The highest summit is about 100 feet above *Chautauqua Lake*, that is, about 1,408 feet, and the soil is a gravelly loam, a rich soil characterized by a mix of sand and clay together with decaying organic materials.

It is a beautiful area with many trees. Those that grow there naturally include *sycamore, birch, elm,* and *sugar maple.* Shrub-like *osier willows* are also found along the creek, but they were imported by the leaders of the Harmonia community in the 1850s with the goal of using their branches to make wicker baskets.

There is more to the valley than simply what one can see and measure. It is a place to be experienced. For those who take time to open their hearts, minds, and senses to this beautiful valley, it can seem a mystical place indeed. As noted in the Introduction, I wrote a good deal of my book, *Holy Ground: Celtic Christian Spirituality,* in this place. Some of the last few sentences of the book were inspired by the valley, and, if I may humbly say so, they are among the best words I have ever written:

> *As I write these words, it is early summer. The woods around me are full of a dazzling celebration of the color green: the emerald richness of maple leaves; the deep green of pine trees; the olives, lime-greens, and yellow-greens of the grass and brush. Overhead a dense canopy of tree branches keeps me dry even during a gentle rain. The stream with its lilting music wanders by our deck. With some imagination I can picture myself at an early Celtic Christian monastery...*[1]

Obviously, I found the valley to be visually inspiring. In addition, it has hidden wonders.

One day in my first year summering there, friends from out-of-town visited. The couple brought with them their youngest son, Justin. I had always found him to be an interesting child (and today he is an interesting college student). Something about the way he would hop around one moment and be dashing off pell mell the next reminded me of the explosive energy of a dragon fly.

Justin bounded out of the car that day and before I knew what was happening he scrambled down the steep ten-foot rocky embankment to the creek. If I had tried to do that myself, I am sure I would have broken an arm or leg. When I dashed to the top of the bank and peered over, Justin was happy and healthy, leaping along the creek from one exposed flat stone to the next. His parents reassured me that he had done that many times when they had camped there in the past.

A few minutes later, Justin was back, looking for a plastic container. I figured he had found some pollywogs, so I scrounged in the cupboard and gave him something to use. Off again, this young dragonfly boy disappeared over the lip of the creek.

In a short time, he returned and showed me his find. I was astonished by what I saw! In the container was a little creature looking like something from a children's story book. Only after showing it to Justin's parents did I learn it was a salamander. I had seen the creature before in science texts, but had never seen one alive right before my eyes and did not know at first what I was seeing. Only much later, after doing some research, did I learn that it was most likely a red salamander, *pseudotriton ruber* being its species name. This little creature has short legs and a tail and usually lives in both woodlands and meadows that are situated near a body of water. It has yellow eyes and its black-spotted body can range in a variety of dazzling colors including red, coral, orange, brown, and purple. All I knew that afternoon, was that I had been introduced to this fascinating creature, up close and personal, by a boy who seemed to defy gravity.

The Kiantone Valley has a considerable variety of creatures roaming about, in addition to humans and salamanders. The fauna list includes the following:

Birds:	wild turkey, blue heron, osprey, ruffled grouse, bald eagle, various song birds
Amphibians:	spiny softshell turtle, redbacked salamander, dusky salamander, tadpole

Mammals:	deer, beaver, raccoon, weasel, striped skunk, opossum, muskrat, fox
Reptiles:	northern redbelly snake, northern ringneck snake
Fish:	darters (several kinds), suckers, minnows
Insects:	dragonflies, black flies, mosquitoes

The valley is the home of these animals. People come, build their structures, erect their tents, park their recreational vehicles, but the valley is still the creatures' home.

I remember a delightful family of wild turkeys that each day put on a morning parade. The father turkey led the way, strutting proudly. Five little baby turkeys toddled behind him. Finally, mother turkey brought up the rear, looking out for stragglers and encouraging them all to follow their dad. They would come across the grove behind our summer home, cross the dirt road, proceed over the wood chip lawn to the high bank of the creek and then follow the bank until they reached a more gradually sloped jumping off spot. Then over the brink they would go, each turkey, big and small, disappearing down to the creek for whatever tasty treat awaited them there. It was a morning ritual not to be missed, especially since it usually took place just at first light when fog still hung over the creek. The turkeys always reminded me of prehistoric creatures emerging out of the mist of early morning, just like a scene from the *Jurassic Park* movies.

I had read and heard much about the *Kiantone Springs*, one of the sources of the creek, before I actually visited them. Many different descriptions and names have been attributed to the springs such as *Sulfur Springs, Deer Lick Springs, Magnetic Springs, and Celtic Springs*. The Native Americans believed they had healing powers and brought their sick and infirm to the springs for treatment. Others considered the waters to have magical powers. The springs played a central role in the development of the Harmonia Spiritualist community.

There are actually several springs located in the Kiantone Valley. They are in close proximity to each other. The water coming from them is strongly alkaline and emits a slight sulfurous smell and taste. The flow of water has never been nor is now very strong. This is why the Kiantone Creek, whose major source of water is the springs and not rain or show-melt runoff, does not overflow very often.

During the years I had a summer home in the Kiantone Valley, I did not take advantage of visiting the Kiantone Springs. I was told the owner of the campground could walk me up the often dry creek bed to the springs, but arthritic knees kept me from accepting that offer. Finally, in the Spring of 2005, I had the opportunity to view the springs first hand. The visit was arranged by Mel Feather, a history teacher who retired not long ago from the Frewsburg Central School system. The springs are located on private property owned by John Kost, an area resident. Mr. Kost inherited the land from his father, who purchased it from Gerald Staples, a retired Jamestown City Court Clerk.

A friend of mine and I visited Mr. Kost in late April when the woods were still full of snowmelt. It was a very rainy day and cold. Mr. Kost unlocked the chain he keeps stretched across the Sturdevant Road entrance to his property which is posted with *No Trespassing* signs. From this spot, which is actually located in Pennsylvania, we descended on a dirt road towards his cabin. The road had many sharp twists and turns. Finally, we reached the cabin where Mr. Kost amicably greeted us and invited us to sit on his enclosed front porch. We talked a bit about the valley, particularly about the Harmonia community. Mr. Kost told us that his property, which also includes a tunnel dug into the sharp hillside by early settlers in search of treasures, has been owned by relatively few people. I quickly sensed that both he and the previous owners had maintained a protective sense toward the property due to the dangers posted by the sharply slanted hillsides, the springs, which literally pop out of the hillsides, and the abandoned tunnel.

Mr. Kost did, however, point out from his porch where two of the springs were located as well as the entrance to the tunnel and the approximate place on the hillside which marked where a large room in the tunnel was located. We chatted with him a while longer, and then took our leave.

At first, I was a bit disappointed with the visit. Although I would have liked to examine the various sites more closely, I understood that Mr. Kost is both wise and prudent to prohibit any scampering up and down the dangerous hillside. In the coming weeks, I also realized that our visit there was like so many other aspects of the Kiantone Valley history. That is, I was left with more questions than answers.

It is no surprise that today, the valley is also known by the name *Hidden Valley*. There is a mystery there and maybe that is the way it is meant to be. But, like a strong itch, I just had to scratch it a little bit more.

CHAPTER 2

CORNPLANTER

THE HEALER OF KIANTONE

I grew up in the 1950s and 1960s with parents who were always very interested in what was happening in the greater world around them. My father had a passion for history and my mother's favorite subject was geography. In addition, every evening meal included a lengthy discussion of current events. The overall environment for these discussions in the 1950s was the *Eisenhower Era*, and in the 1960s it was the *Viet Nam War*. There are three particular events of which I have vivid memories of my parents' reactions and discussions. The first was the 1962 *Cuban Missile Crisis*. The second was *President Kennedy's assassination* in 1963. The third was the *relocation of Chief Cornplanter's grave by the Army Corp of Engineers* in 1964.

I shared these recollections with another baby-boomer friend over lunch one day. He nodded when I mentioned Cuba, JFK, the Eisenhower years, and Viet Nam, and I knew instantly that those events shaped his family's dinner conversations, too. But when I recalled *Cornplanter*, he looked up from his *noodle chow mai fun* with a blank stare. Quickly, I gave him a synopsis of the Cronplanter story.

Cornplanter was a *Seneca Indian* whose life spanned the late 18th and early 19th centuries. During the *American Revolution* he and his tribe fought with the *British* against the American colonists. But, after the war, Pennsylvania gave Cornplanter three large tracts of land in Western Pennsylvania in gratitude for his assistance with Indian affairs. *George Washington* told Cornplanter that he and his descendents could own the lands as long as the *Allegheny River* ran, a rather poetic way for Washington seemingly to imply *forever.* Cornplanter eventually sold two of the land grants, but retained the one located approximately two miles south of the New York and Pennsylvania border beside the Allegheny River. With great confidence in Washington's promise, Cornplanter lived out his days on the remaining land grant and was buried there.

About 130 years later, the *Army Corps of Engineers* decided that the remaining land grant area, along with lands owned by *White Anglo* residents, needed to be flooded by a dam designed to protect towns, cities, and businesses along the Allegheny River flood plain. The dam created by the Army Corps of Engineers would make the river *cease running,* so-to-speak. In reaction, many Senecas and others believed that President Washington's great promise to Cornplanter and his descendants was broken. The Seneca living on the grant were relocated, and Cornplanter's grave was moved from the original site to *Riverside Cemetery,* located on the east side of the new reservoir just south of the state line. An excellent account of all this dam business can be found in William N. Hoover's recent book, *Kinzua: from Cornplanter to the Corps.* Many people today, both Seneca and White Anglo alike, consider the moving of Cornplanter's grave to be a sad ending to the stellar saga of one of the greatest Seneca chiefs.

Cornplanter became a chief of the Senecas not by birth but, rather, by strength of character. He was born *circa* 1750 near *Avon, NY,* about 27 miles southwest of *Rochester, NY* (Map 2), and died February 18, 1836 at home on his land grant in *Warren County, PA.* His father was *John O'Bail* and he was part of a prominent *Dutch American* family in the *Albany, NY* area. John's Dutch family name

New York
State

LAKE ONTARIO

• Niagara Falls • Rochester
• Buffalo • AVON

Syracuse

• Rome

• Utica

• Albany

LAKE
ERIE

• Jamestown

Elmira •

Plattsburg •

Map 2

New
York
City •

was *Abeel,* but was corrupted to *O'Bail* because it sounded more Irish than Dutch.

Cornplanter's father made his way to the frontier, then located in Western New York, where he found work as a trader and gun-smith. He made good friends with the *Iroquois* tribes because he knew how to repair the firearms the French and British had given to them in return for their allegiance and support. It was on this frontier that John O'Bail courted and then married Cornplanter's mother, a prominent member of the *Wolf Clan.* She was a Seneca of the *Iroquois Confederacy.* Suffice it to say that Cornplanter was blessed with unique and influential birth parents on both sides of the family. John O'Bail eventually left his Seneca family and mar-ried a White Anglo woman by whom he had several children. This leaving behind a Native American family and marrying a White Anglo woman was common on the frontier. O'Bail and other fron-tiersmen believed there was nothing illegal about this, but that is an understanding that denies and denigrates Native American traditions and rituals.

As noted above, Cornplanter became a Seneca chief not by birth, but by his exemplary leadership of his people. The Senecas sided with the British in the fight against the American Colonists. Among their many warriors, it was Cornplanter who shined as both ferocious and effective. He took many scalps and brutally tortured many prisoners to death. Following that war, however, Cornplanter almost immediately assumed the role of an eloquent diplomat and statesman on behalf of the Senecas, as well as the other nations of the Iroquois Confederacy, which included the *Ca-yuga, Onondaga, Oneida, Mohawk,* and the *Tuscarora Native Americans.* In 1789, Cornplanter negotiated with the Iroquois and kept them from joining the Native Americans in the *Old Northwest Territory.* These Native Americans were fighting against the settlers who wished to locate to *Ohio* and other sections of the territory that eventually were incorporated into the states of *Indiana, Illinois, Michigan, Wisconsin,* and part of *Minnesota.* Because of Cornplanter's ability to keep the Senecas out of the fighting, the settlers prevailed against the resisting indigenous Native Americans. One interpretation of this is that Cornplanter recognized a losing battle and sued for peace on behalf of his people.

In 1791, the *Pennsylvania General Assembly* gave Cornplanter three tracts of land, totaling 640 acres. Note that these were land grants, not reservations, and were intended for Cornplanter's use and also for him to pass on to his descendants. The grants were given in recognition and appreciation for his diplomatic work, specifically, "for valuable services to the whites",[2] the words in quotation marks actually quoted from the original document giving Cornplanter the grants. By 1794, the Iroquois Confederacy had been subdued by the United States through treaties and the tribes were placed on reservations. Cornplanter and his family and heirs, however, lived out their lives on his land grants, land they believed rightfully belonged to Cornplanter and his descendants.

It is not surprising that after the American Revolution, Cornplanter played a mediating, healing role, especially since he was well aware of his bi-racial background. There is one remarkable account that tells of an encounter during a Revolutionary War battle in which Cornplanter's father, fighting with the American Colonists, was taken prisoner by the Senecas. Cornplanter recognized his father, but the father was unaware of his son's presence. As Hoover cites in his excellent book referred to above, Cornplanter introduced himself to his father and offered to either enfold the father into Cornplanter's tribe and take care of his every need, or return the man safely to his new family under the banner of a Seneca security detail. The father chose his new family and was safely returned to them. This was one of many times when Cornplanter exhibited his compassionate and healing nature.

11

The name Cornplanter is pronounced either *Gyant-wa-hia* or *Gy-ant-wa-cha* in the Seneca language. It means *One Who Plants* or *By What One Plants*. This is because of the work Cornplanter did with the *Quakers* in the last years of the 18th Century and the early 19th Century. In 1798, Cornplanter invited Quakers he had met in Philadelphia to come to his land grants. If nothing else, Cornplanter was a manager of change. He saw the many changes taking place around his people because of the coming of the white settlers and their way of life. He knew that these changes could either bring final defeat to the Senecas or become the means by which they could adapt to the new political, economic, and social climate. At Cornplanter's specific request, the Quakers provided assistance and training in education, farming, and construction. In fact, with the Quaker's assistance, Cornplanter became an agricultural teacher among all the Iroquois. This was a leader who was vitally interested in his people's well-being. Cornplanter, seeing the damage alcohol abuse could bring to a community, also eventually worked in the *Temperance Movement* even though he later lost interest in it.

And so, it is this man, this Cornplanter, *Gyant-wa-hia,* the one who is a peacemaker, leader, and healer of his people, who brings to Kiantone Springs the sick and the infirm. The springs were not located on one of Cornplanter's land grants. But, this was in those last years before the White Anglo settlers would come and purchase the land for their own restricted use. In the late 1700s, the Senecas still roamed freely along the Allegheny, the Conewango, and their tributaries. Knowing about him as we do, it is easy to imagine this reportedly handsome man of Dutch and Seneca descent, walking steadily through the deep woods, mindful of the infirmities some of his followers bear, but intent on taking them to a place where they might be nurtured and healed.

Thus, as early as 1785, some of the first settlers in Warren County, PA knew of the reported healing properties of waters in the Kiantone Springs, located just across the border in New York State. Frontier settlers relayed tales of how they saw the Senecas, led by Cornplanter, bringing their aged and sick to the Kiantone Springs for healing. Did the springs really have healing properties (and do they today?), or were these treks simply wishful thinking on the compassionate chief's part? One can only answer that question by faith. Still, the springs, even then, did have a mystical background that could easily lead one to consider them having curative powers.

One of Cornplanter's land grants, named, *The Gift,* was located in present day *Oil City, PA* (Map 3). Cornplanter and his people used the oil found there for medicinal purposes. Later, when some White Anglo settlers purchased that land grant from him, Cornplanter felt he was swindled out of an important land holding. Today's official Oil City website mentions Cornplanter's presence, but makes no mention of the oil's curative properties. If the Oil City White Anglos were ever aware of the oil's healing potential, that story was overshadowed in 1859 by the drilling of *Drake's Oil Well* in nearby *Titusville, PA,* the first such engineering feat in the world. It should be noted, however, that in 2001 the *Oil City Arts Council* dedicated a six-foot bronze statue of Cornplanter (see cover of this book) in the *Creekside Park,* along *Oil Creek* in downtown Oil City, and in 2002, published an excellent pamphlet, *Cornplanter Was Here: The Story of a Seneca Chief's Legacy to Oil City.*

In the 1800s, the legacy of Cornplanter lingered on in the hearts and minds of both the Senecas and the new White Anglo settlers. Even the *Civil War,* which badly disrupted American society in the 1860s, could not dispel the memories of this great leader. The grieving nation was busy dedicating and adorning large cemeteries where the Civil War dead had fallen in places like *Gettysburg*

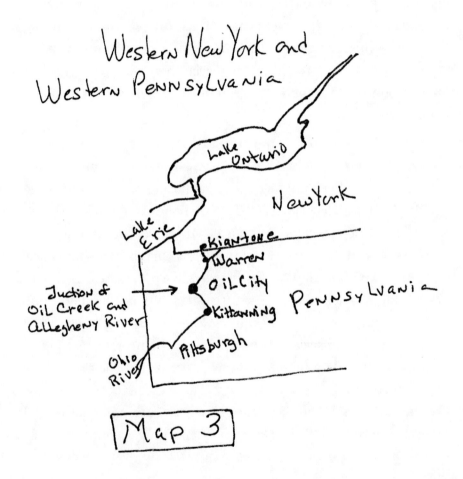

Western New York and
Western Pennsylvania

Lake Ontario

New York

Lake Erie

Kiantone

Warren

Juction of
Oil Creek and
Allegheny River

Oil City

Kittanning   Pennsylvania

Ohio River

Pittsburgh

Map 3

and *Antietam*. And, yet, in 1866, the *Pennsylvania General Assembly erected America's first monument intended to honor a Native American,* the statesman and healer named Cornplanter. The monument, located at the chief's original burial site and moved to Riverside Cemetery in 1964, held the following proclamation on the its west side:

Chief of the Seneca Tribe, and a principal Chief of the Six Nations,

from the period of the Revolutionary War to the time of his death.

Distinguished for talents, courage, eloquence and sobriety,

and love of his tribe and race,

to whose welfare he devoted his time,

his energy and his means,

during a long and eventful life.

CHAPTER 3

Early Settlers
White Anglo Pioneers

Jamestown, NY and the surrounding countryside, including Kiantone, are noted for their many trees. Sometimes in mid-summer, particularly in July when the trees are in full foliage, they hide many of the buildings and homes from view. At those times, I have tried to imagine what the area looked like before settlers arrived and cleared so much of the land. I do know that they came to an area covered with primeval forest. It was so dense that a man riding a horse through it could not journey without the danger of being knocked off his saddle by tree branches or having his way blocked by the dense tree growth.

The early White Anglo settlers to Kiantone Creek and the surrounding area were drawn by the availability of tillable land and flowing water. Though much of it first needed to be cleared of timber, there was plenty of land for growing grain and grazing animals. The Conewango Creek ran through the area and also connected to the Allegheny River at present day *Warren, PA*. The Allegheny was used as a major waterway for keelboat operators who brought foodstuffs, whiskey, and other supplies north from *Pittsburgh*. Both Stillwater Creek, a wider stream located about two miles north of Kiantone Creek and flowing into the Conewango Creek, and Kiantone Creek, while not usually rushing torrents, presented enough water to be dammed for sawmills.

Kiantone was first settled by *Joseph L. Akin* in 1807. The area consisted of about 11,228 acres (roughly 17.5 square miles). Akin came from *Rensselaer County*, a county in eastern New York located on the Hudson River near Troy and Albany. That county dates back to 1630, when it was part of the Van Rensselaer patron holdings of the *Dutch West India Company*. Moving from this relatively established area to the frontier of Western New York, Akin settled on Stillwater Creek.

Not long after, another settler, *Robert Russell*, came to the area. He partnered with *John Frew* to build the first sawmill on Kiantone Creek just above the junction where the creek met the Conewango Creek. It should be noted that *Russell, PA*, located on the Conewango Creek just a few miles south of Kiantone, was settled by Russell and his father and brothers in 1800.

The name, *Kiantone*, was a derivative of the Seneca word, *Kyenthone (or Kyenthono* in some sources) and meant, roughly, *level place for growing corn*. Most likely, it referred to the area where the Kiantone Creek met the Conewango Creek, extending on level ground along each creek. It was not the first official name of the White Anglo settlement, but came into use later in association with the Kiantone Creek name. It also appears as *"Kyenthono, a Small Indian Town"*, on a 1787 map created by surveyors who measured and mapped the New York State and Pennsylvania line.[3]

In 1794, the Senecas received exclusive rights to reservation lands, made possible by the diplomatic efforts of Chief Cornplanter and others. But they did not suddenly move *en masse* to the reservations, as the transition was more gradual in some, but not all areas of the state. Some historical sources seem to indicate that when the White Anglo settlers first arrived in Kiantone to live on land they purchased from the *Holland Land Company*, they found the *Kyenthono* Seneca village still inhabited, or at least used by

Senecas for growing corn. No doubt the Senecas took note of the increased keelboat activity that surely involved shipping lumber south to the Allegheny River and beyond as well as the shipping of necessary goods upstream to the saw mill on the Kiantone Creek.

Akin divided the land into lots but would not sell them to other newcomers. Instead, he offered long-term leases for those who would improve the land. Akin brought this lease system with him from Rensselaer County. It was, however, an unpopular business arrangement for settlers who preferred to purchase and own the land. The few buildings built during this time in what was unofficially dubbed, *Akinsville*, included two houses, one belonging to Laban Case who operated a tavern in the building, and a blacksmith shop. It appears that in the early years the hamlet was located near the Kiantone Creek, although today the hamlet is better located as being in the vicinity of the *Kiantone Congregational Church*.

Akin's nearby competitor on *The Rapids* (Map 4)[4] a swift flowing section of Chautauqua Lake's *Outlet*, was *James Predergast*, a lumberman and mill builder. Prendergast was deeded 1,000 acres from his brother, *Martin*, and purchased additional acreage along the Outlet on which to build his own businesses as well as to sell outright to other settlers. Most hardy pioneers decided that, if they were going to put their sweat equity into the land, then they wanted to own it, too. Therefore, Prendergast's settlement, which became Jamestown, founded in 1811, prospered and Akinsville did not. In time, James Prendergast developed a large homestead in Kiantone which he passed on to his son, *Alexander T. Prendergast*, who developed it into a model farm *still* in operation today.

Settlers who came to the area (Map 2 and 4) either came up the Allegheny River from Pittsburgh or came overland from *Buffalo, NY*

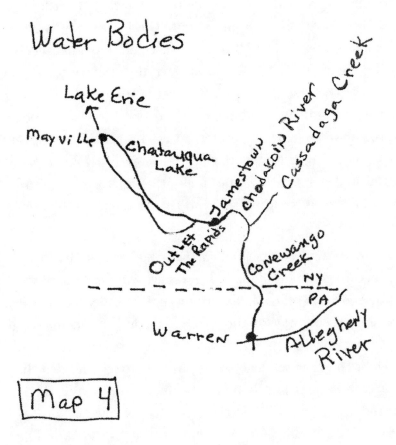

Water Bodies

or from eastern New York State by wagon. Those traveling from Buffalo came down the *Buffalo-Erie Road* (actually more of an old Indian trail than a road) to *The Crossroads*, a settlement established in 1802 and eventually renamed, *Westfield*. Here their journey took a left-hand turn as they entered the winding *Portage Trail* that had been cut into the ridge rising between *Barcelona Harbor* and the head of *Chautauqua Lake*, located at 1,308 feet above sea level. The ridge was the hydrological dividing place. Waters that ran to the west flowed to *Lake Erie*, the *Niagara River* including its majestic falls, into *Lake Ontario* and then into the *St. Lawrence River* and, eventually, the *Atlantic Ocean*. Waters flowing east-southeast ran into Chautauqua Lake and its Outlet, the *Chadakoin* River, the Conewango Creek[5], the Allegheny River and then into the *Ohio River* and the *Mississippi River*, finally emptying into the *Gulf of Mexico*. Thus, the Portage Trail traversed strategic ground for a society dependent on water travel. This nine-mile trail was cut by the French explorer, *Pierre Joseph Celeron de Blainville*, in 1749. It was part of *France's* attempt to secure the area and establish an overland route from Lake Erie to *Fort Dusquene* (today's Pittsburgh), and thus secure France's claims west of the *Allegheny Mountains*.

The early pioneers' journey over the Portage Trail ended in *Mayville*, another frontier settlement established in 1804. From the head of Chautauqua Lake, keelboat operators transported new settlers, supplies, and other items down the lake to the Outlet, 17.5 miles to the southeast. *Keelboats* were sturdy wooden craft moved by as many as eight men on each side simultaneously inserting long poles into the water until they touched bottom, thus using leverage as a propulsion system. A rudder operator at the rear of the keelboat assisted in navigation. Many keelboats were large enough to have a crude cabin running lengthwise down the center of the vessel.

Growing up in *Ashville*, one mile southwest of Chautauqua Lake, I have seen the lake in its many faces which vary depending on the weather conditions. On a hot summer day, it can lie calm and stunningly blue. Windy days bring rough white caps. Cold wintry days often arrive in late October or early November. Occurring before the lake ices over, they bring a foreboding look of deep copenhagen blue to the lake surface, often with choppy waves caused by fierce late autumn winds. This last image of the lake sets the backdrop for the next settler that arrived in the Kiantone area and the arrival of his young family a few months later.

Solomon Jones arrived from *Wardsboro, VT* in 1810. During the summer, he cleared woods on his lot and erected the shell of a log house. In the autumn, he returned to Vermont and retrieved his family. Then, as winter approached, they traveled together to Mayville. There Jones hired a keelboat to take his wife and five daughters on the two-day trip down Chautauqua Lake to The Rapids (Map 4). If that sounds daunting enough, consider that his daughters were age nine and younger!

Meanwhile, Jones and his oldest child, *Ellick*, brought their horses overland down the east side of the lake where corn stubble was available for the animals. The boat journey took place during terribly cold days, with frigid waves spraying and splashing the mother and her young children. When the keelboat reached the Outlet they found it was frozen over, stopping further passage of the keelboat to The Rapids. Having delivered their human cargo as far as seemingly possible, the boatmen returned on foot to Mayville. The men, astonishingly, left the mother and girls alone on the keelboat either to wait for the father and son to find them or somehow continue on their own. Left alone, they chose to chop ice so that the keelboat could pass through the Outlet where snow covered the ground on both sides of the waterway. There appears to be no record of how the mother and very young daughters dealt physically and emotionally with this ordeal. But to me, it seems as though the journey must have been both exhausting and terrifying.

Once reunited, the Jones family continued traveling to Kiantone and moved into the log cabin, which had no chimney, on November 16, 1810. After the long winter, Jones became a corn and potato farmer. Their journey to present-day Kiantone was not quite as horrifying as that of California's *Donner Party*, but it most certainly was retold to the family's children and grandchildren for decades.

Another early settler to the Kiantone area, *Jasper Marsh*, was a farmer and a mechanic. He made large spinning wheels, reels, common chairs, hay rakes, fork handles and other lathe-made wooden articles for area settlers. These he stamped with his name, "J. Marsh", using a hot iron.

In 1811, *William Martin*, a *Universalist* by faith and a temperance worker by commitment, settled in the area. He allowed no whiskey on his farm for his workers, even though that was the custom at the time. In William Martin, also known as Captain William Martin, we see another aspect of early settler life in Kiantone and the entire Chautauqua County region. The United States of America, at that time, were[6] engaged in the *War of 1812*. The threat from British soldiers stationed at *Fort Niagara* near the Niagara River's inlet into Lake Ontario was real and present. Captain Martin served in the war as an ensign for *Lieutenant William Forbes* in 1813. On the same day that the British burned Buffalo, he was taken prisoner on *Black Rock Road*, a New York State road that ran along the Niagara River just beyond its emergence from Lake Erie and roughly parallel to today's *Interstate 490*. Martin was subsequently imprisoned in *Montreal, Canada*, until May 14, 1814. He was eventually released from active duty, but then was called out again in the autumn and became a captain.

This account of Captain Martin's wartime activities cites the details, but does not consider the emotional roller coaster of his military service. Captain Martin was called to help defend a critical strategic site of the War of 1812, the relatively narrow Niagara River that separated the British and American frontlines. He experienced the British soldiers breaching this river boundary, the battle that ensued, and the frustration of becoming a prisoner of war. His journey to imprisonment in Montreal was probably by ship across Lake Ontario and down the St. Lawrence River. We can only imagine the dire conditions of his confinement. Somehow, he was eventually released and made his way back to Kiantone, only to be called to military service once again. History books and articles do not provide all the details of Captain Martin's military experience. Suffice it to say, however, that people like him in Kiantone were living frontier lives that were full of both personal trials and the challenge of securing their nation's future.

Captain Martin had three grandsons who served, many years later, in the *Civil War*. Living well past the end of that conflict, Captain Martin died September 13, 1875. His long life encompassed the era of Cornplanter, the early settlement of Kiantone, the War of 1812, the decades-long abolitionist struggle, the Harmonia Spiritualist community, the Civil War and its aftermath. How I wish he had written an autobiography or at least kept a detailed diary of his reactions and interactions with all he experienced in his life!

William Sears (1788-1827), also from Wardsboro, VT, came to the Kiantone settlement in 1811, the same year as William Martin. Sears had married *Ruth Cheney* in 1808, whose parents also came to Kiantone in 1811. They traveled 500 miles overland by oxen drawn sled, brining their household goods with them. Sears, a relatively young 23-year-old, opened a tavern just north of Kiantone Creek. Eventually, his enterprises expanded to two taverns and a hotel, signifying some considerable libation and housing activity in the area. It is noteworthy that William and Ruth's son, *Clinton W.*, was educated at *Yale* and *Wesleyan University*.

Elijah Braley (1787-1864) also came from Wardboro, VT in 1811. He was from a family of 12 children and his father, *Lemuel Braley*, was an excellent farmer and distinguished deacon of the *Wardboro Baptist Church*. Elijah married *Lucinda*, daughter of *Ebenezer* and *Jane (White) Sears* in 1810 and, presumably, brought her with him to Kiantone. She died in 1817, probably of one of the typical pioneer causes of death: giving birth, sickness, or malnutrition, or some combination of the three.

It is interesting to note that Lemuel Braley and Ebenezer Sears were the first two deacons in the Wardboro, VT Baptist Church. Lucinda's brother was William Sears, therefore, Elijah Braley was William Sears' brother-in-law. These and many other families came from Wardsboro, VT to the area of Kiantone.[7]

In 1812 or 1818 (the actual date is disputable), *Ebenezer Davis*, a settler from Vermont, was recorded as the first person baptized in Stillwater Creek at *Akin's Bridge*. One can imagine the spectators gathered on the bridge and creek side to watch the event.

Also, in 1812, *James Hall*, again, from Wardsboro, VT, arrived. Evidently, he became a well respected citizen because in 1833, he was elected as a Democrat member of the *New York State Assembly*. Hall had the distinction of marrying three of the Cheney daughters. They were the daughters of Ebenezer Cheney, a distinguished American Revolutionary War soldier who saw action at *Bunker Hill*, *Bennington*, and *Saratoga*. Mr. Cheney began a successful farming dynasty in Kiantone that as late as 1955, was cited by the *New York State Agricultural Society* as a *Century Farm*. Hall managed to marry the series of Cheney daughters because the first two died before he finally married the healthy third sister. Given the poor state of medical care at that time, this probably was not as unusual an occurrence as it would be today. With his first wife, *Mary*, Hall had three children, *Abigail, Lewis,* and *Eliel*. He and his second wife, *Abigail*, had no children. With the healthy wife, *Maria*, Hall fathered three children, *Erie, Mary,* and *James*.

It should be noted that through his marrying the various Cheney sisters, James Hall became related to Elijah Braley and William Sears. There is a tendency to think of American pioneers setting out for the frontier, never to see *kith and kin* again. Obviously, this was not necessarily so. Groups of people, particularly, but not always, younger people, did set out in community groups together. Sometimes, they brought along the older folks, knowing they might die on the journey, but simply because the older folks could not bear to be left behind. One strong advantage to pioneers grouping together from their former communities was that they knew each others' skills, experience, and, perhaps, even their foibles. Thus, they were able to form a stronger unit on the frontier.

Samuel Garfield arrived in 1814. Garfield, a carpenter and farmer, found an ingenious way to combine both specialties. He made half-bushel and smaller dry measures and invented a process of making scythe snaths by steaming and bending. Garfield eventually produced several thousand snaths per year, shipping them south and west, until all the ash timber in the Kiantone area had been exhausted.

It is worthwhile to look at the evolution of community names in the Kiantone area. In Upstate and Western New York State, each major governmental section within a county is officially called a *town*. A town may include a *village*, as in the Village of Frewsburg, or a *city*, as in the City of Jamestown. The word, *town*, is also used informally to describe a community somewhat larger than a village, such as a *county seat*, and occasionally even a city, especially when used as *downtown*. A *hamlet* is an unincorporated village, that is, a tiny village that turns to the town government for supervision and the organizing of its governmental community life.

Kiantone, with its various names, as already noted and described below, has always been a hamlet. The name of the town in which the hamlet exists, however, changed several times during the 1800s. It was first located in the Town of Pomfret, then assigned to the Town of Ellicott in 1812, then the Town of Carroll in 1825, and finally to the Town of Kiantone in 1853 (Map 1). The hamlet itself was first known informally as Akinsville, then Sears, then Searsville, then Carroll, and, finally, Kiantone, as it is known today. Generally speaking, throughout this book I have referred to *Kiantone* and the *Town of Kiantone* to describe the locations noted, regardless of time period.

Benjamin Jones settled in the area in 1815. On August 24, 1821, he received an appointment to establish a post office six miles south of Jamestown. He operated the office out of his home, which in time became the Cheney homestead. The post office name was *Fairbank* (1821), then changed to *Carroll* in 1826, and, finally, to *Kiantone* in 1855. It closed in 1900.

The Reverend John Spencer organized the first *Congregational Church* in Kiantone in 1815. This congregation went through various name change and will be examined again in Chapter 10. The church's first meeting house was built in 1830 on land given by William Sears' widow. Previously, the congregation met in homes and school houses. The original congregation consisted of five male and five female members.

Ezbai Kidder, also from Wardsboro, VT, came to Kiantone in 1816. In 1854, he became the first supervisor of the Town of Kiantone, which today is the smallest township in Chautauqua County. Other settlers continued to come as the first part of the 19th Century unfolded. In 1830, *Ebenezer Chapin* settled on the southeast side of what was then the Town of Carroll, later the Town of Kiantone. He had seven children. Another early settler in the area was *Roderick Chapin*, from Warsaw, New York, who died in 1857. He was a preacher in the *Methodist Episcopal Church* and later served in the *Cumberland Presbyterian* denomination.

All of these early settlers, their wives, and their children and grandchildren faced a daunting task in coming to the Kiantone area. The trip to the area was incredibly hard, as noted above with the account of the Jones, Sears, and Cheney families. Once on site, they lived in primitive log houses. Food was either raised as vegetables, harvested from native apple trees and berry bushes, hunted as game, or purchased at a dear price from the keelboats that came upriver from Pittsburgh. In time, grain was planted and grist mills built, but producing flour and cereals this way was no easy task. Alcohol, for those who imbibed, was hard to come by and had to be either purchased from the keelboat operators who sold whiskey or made by hand from locally grown apples or grain. Some say that as many apples found their way into *applejack*, a homemade alcoholic beverage, as they did into apple pies! There was hardly any medical care aside from folk medicine remedies, including those learned from the Senecas.

The *Erie Canal* was completed in 1825, providing, as the song lyrics tell us, mule-hauled packet transportation from Albany in eastern New York State to Buffalo in the west. The canal was, indeed, a remarkable feat for its day. Once completed, life became gradually better for settlers on New York State's western frontier. The terrible loneliness was eased as more settlers arrived. Goods were easier and cheaper to purchase. The early settlers had lived in abject poverty, but as the early middle years of the 1800s approached, the local economy became stronger. More churches were established along with more schools for children and youth. The *Atlantic and Great Western Railroad* arrived in Jamestown on August 30, 1860, to the cheers and amazement of enthusiastic citizens. It was a small train, carrying only a few guests. But it also signaled a significant change in the city and the southern part of Chautauqua County, including Kiantone, linking residents to the *Erie Railroad* system and on to New York City in the east and St. Louis in the west.

All of this progress was encouraging to the early Kiantone settlers. They had worked hard to carve a life out of what to them, unlike the Senecas for whom the area was home, had seemed a daunting wilderness. And just when things began to get a bit better, the distant drums of happenings in far away places began seriously to affect their lives.

CHAPTER 4

DISTANT DRUMS

The Underground Railroad and the Abolition Movement

Currently, I live in Bloomington, a city located in the south-central part of Indiana, about 100 miles north of the Ohio River. One of the cultural aspects that I have adjusted to since coming here five years ago is Indiana's continuing saga of race relations. Although a *free state* in the years leading up to the Civil War, Indiana law stated that runaway slaves could pass through, but not settle and remain in the state.

Approximately 30 years ago, a murder believed to be racially motivated took place in nearby Martinsville, IN. Thus, this community, unfortunately and perhaps undeservedly for many of its citizens, continues to have a poor reputation regarding race relations. I have friends here who, because of their skin color and ethnicity, make it a point never to stop in that small city.

Martinsville is not the only Indiana city to bear the stigma of racial injustice. Bloomington had separate schools for blacks and whites well into the 20th Century. And, on July 4, 1999, a South Korean Indiana University student walking up the sidewalk of the Korean United Methodist Church in Bloomington was murdered by a white supremacist from a nearby state.

Needless to say, all this creates a sense of underlying *dis-ease* in the community and surrounding area. Many Hoosiers, as Indiana

31

folk like to call themselves, faithfully serve in organizations devoted to eliminating racism. However, the issue of racism is always
present in the community's collective conscience.

I share this scenario as a contrasting backdrop to discussing
the culture of Kiantone and the surrounding area (Map 5) in the
years leading up to the Civil War. In the same way that the issue
of racism constantly affects the Bloomington, IN, culture today, in
antebellum Kiantone there were feelings, dangers, and divisions
all focused on the major issue of that community's time in history, namely the issue of slavery. This *dis-ease* was on the minds
of most American citizens at that time, and guided the actions of
many courageous people. The South's institution of slavery was an
edgy and disconcerting reality that the Kiantone folks, one way or
the other, were almost forced to address in both their public and
private lives. This focus on slavery was felt in theological, social,
economic, and political ways.

For example, consider the 1843 split that occurred in the nearby
Jamestown *Methodist Episcopal Church* because that denomination
was reacting to the issue of slavery like the proverbial ostrich with
its head in the sand. Those leaving joined a newly formed *Wesleyan Church* because that denomination had a strong anti-slavery
platform. The Wesleyan Church members based their beliefs on
Bible passages such as St. Paul's proclamation of freedom for slaves
through Christ (Galatians 3:28).

Meanwhile, the Methodist Episcopal denomination struggled
with continued schism in its own ranks, with Methodists in the
South separating from the denomination in 1844 while maintaining some ties such as joint publishing ventures. Northern leaders
of the Methodist Episcopal Church abhorred slavery, but also did
not want to lose the numerous church members in the slave-holding border states. Finally, towards the end of the 1850s, the line

became more clearly drawn between the pro-slavery Methodist Episcopal Church South and the original Methodist Episcopal Church in the North and border states. In 1857, the former Jamestown Methodists who left to join the Wesleyans returned to the fold and reunited with the Methodist Episcopal Church. Surely this church split and reunion, occurring in a major congregation in Jamestown, did not go unnoticed in nearby Kiantone.

In reality, although few in number, slaves had been held in Chautauqua County since the first decades of settlement. But in 1817, New York State passed a law that all slaves had to be freed by July 4, 1827. In 1820, only the Prendergast family still owned slaves. Given the distinguished heritage of this family, the fact that they held slaves is probably both shocking and paradoxical. However, the practice was not uncommon in many regions of the United States in its early history. The Prendergast's freed all their slaves well before the 1827 deadline, thus eliminating the practice of slave-holding in Chautauqua County.

Slavery, as it thereafter existed in the South, continued to generate a moral reaction in Chautauqua County. One positive contribution of some local citizens was to help runaway slaves make their way to freedom. The destination of these slaves was Canada because this British territory had begun a gradual emancipation of slaves in 1793, followed by the total elimination of slavery in all British colonies in 1833. In Canada, many of these newly-freed former slaves found a home at Ontario's *Wilberforce Colony*, an agricultural and educational community founded especially for runaway slaves. It was named after *William Wilberforce*, the British Christian social reformer instrumental in abolishing the British slave trade in 1793, and slavery itself in 1833.

The *Underground Railroad*, also known as the *UGR* or *UGRR*, was active in the Jamestown area in the decades leading up to the Civil

War. It relied on foot traffic, horses, wagons or buggies for transportation and used local residents' homes, cellars, and barns for shelter. The sites were designated by a special code that adopted the language of the railroad. Thus, safe homes and farms were called *stations*, and concerned citizens who facilitated the program were called *agents* and *conductors*. Steamers on Lake Erie and the other *Great Lakes* that transported runaway slaves to freedom in Canada were known as *extensions of the track*.

There were several UGRR routes that snaked their way through both Chautauqua County and its eastern neighbor, *Cattaraugus County*. A constant signpost along the way was the *North Star*, which steered runaway slaves toward Canada and the protection of the British government. In addition to navigating by the North Star, *quilts* were also used to direct the runaway slaves north. In Jacqueline T. Tobin and Raymond G. Dobard's excellent book, *Hidden in Plain View: A Secret Story of Quilts and the Underground Railroad*, the authors describe the development of a quilt code developed to mark the UGRR's routes. Quilters used patterns, such as arrows or zigzag designs, to give directions. The quilts were hung out windows or draped over fence rails, seemingly to air, but, in reality, as signposts for runaway slaves in their journey to freedom.

In Chapter 5 there is a lengthy description of the tunnel constructed by Kiantone residents in the early 1850s. Straddling the New York and Pennsylvania border, it was sometimes reported that this tunnel was used to smuggle escaped slaves from one state to the next. However, this theory about the tunnel does not make much sense. The slaves had already fled over the northern border of the Southern states that maintained slavery, namely every state south of the Mason Dixon Line and the Ohio River. Neither Pennsylvania nor New York were, by this time, slave-holding states. It is far more likely that the Kiantone tunnel was simply used as a place to hide slaves until they could be safely moved under the cover of night.

Many Chautauqua County residents participated in abolitionist activities. An *Anti-Slavery County Convention* was held in 1845. In 1856, a *Ladies' Fugitive Aid Society* was initiated with a meeting held on July 4. The purpose of this group was to aid runaway slaves.

Anti-slavery activities were not limited to the Jamestown and Chautauqua County areas. In fact, Kiantone was surrounded by neighbors in both New York and Pennsylvania who were also devoted to this work. *Robert Falconer* lived in nearby *Sugar Grove, PA*, eight miles west of Kiantone and located just south of the state line. Mr. Falconer was a Scottish immigrant who was the area's largest landowner along the New York and Pennsylvania border. He owned mills in Warren and *Franklin, PA*, as well as in *Kennedy* and *Falconer, NY*. Mr. Falconer made a fortune while controlling the cotton trade between *Charleston, SC* and *Scotland*. His wealth, however, did not keep him from seeing the horrors of slavery first-hand. Falconer was appalled by slavery and in 1831 signed a petition that called for ending slavery in the *District of Columbia*.

Other residents living not far from Kiantone were also involved in the abolition movement, which continued to strengthen throughout the 1830s, 1840s, and 1850s. *Dr. James Catlan*, another Sugar Grove resident, was a celebrated founder of several hydrotherapy hospitals. He also published the *True American*, an anti-slavery newspaper.

Frederick Miles, son of the first Sugar Grove area settler, brought the renowned abolitionist, *Frederick Douglass*, to tea at his sister-in-law's home located about one-half mile south of the New York and Pennsylvania line on the *Big Tree-Sugar Grove Road*. The home was owned by *Cynthia Catlan Miller*. She was an ardent abolitionist who founded both the *Female Assisting Society* and the *Ladies Fugitive Aid Society*.

There is little doubt that the abolitionist fires of Mrs. Miller and others in Sugar Grove were fueled by an *abolitionist convention*, the largest ever recorded in the area with hundreds attending. It was held at the *Yonnie Farmstead* in Sugar Grove in 1854. At that time, there was a campaign to hold 100 similar conventions across the United States Northeast and Midwest regions. Frederick Douglasss was a keynote speaker at the Sugar Grove convention and also deemed that event to be the best of all the abolition conventions.

Lansing Wetmore was another local abolitionist who lived to the southeast of Kiantone just across the border in Pennsylvania's *Conewango Township*. In 1831, Mr. Lansing, who would one day become a Warren County judge, joined with Robert Falconer and signed the call for ending slavery in the District of Columbia. *Mrs. Isaac Hilliar* was a leader of the *Conewango Township Ladies Assisting Society* in 1856. This group sewed clothing which was sent to the Quakers in Philadelphia for distribution to runaway slaves. Further south in Warren, PA, about 13 miles south of Kiantone, the *Honorable Glenn Schofield*, a member of the *United States House of Representatives*, made frequent anti-slavery speeches.

All of this abolitionist activity took place in a rough triangle surrounding Kiantone that contained approximately 75 square miles (Map 5). Surely, it had a profound effect on Kiantone residents and many of them were probably involved in the activities cited.

In addition, much of Upstate and Western New York (Map 2) was the scene of zealous abolitionist endeavors. With the assistance of *Harriet Tubman*, Rochester became a main station on the UGR. Near Fredonia, UGR Agent *Dr. James Pettit* operated a station

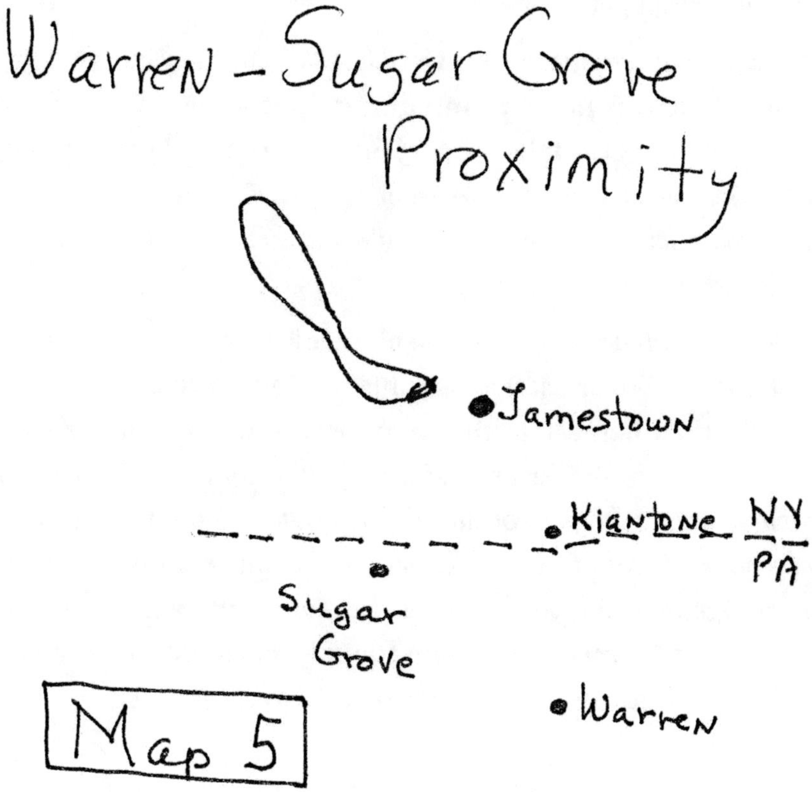

Warren – Sugar Grove Proximity

● Jamestown

- - - - - - - - - ● Kiantone $\frac{NY}{PA}$

● Sugar Grove

Map 5

● Warren

for nearly 25 years at Versailles in Cattaraugus County on the banks of *Cattaraugus Creek*, a tributary of Lake Erie. *Sketches in the History of the Underground Railroad* is his collected reminiscences commissioned by the editors of the *Fredonia Censor* and published by that newspaper in 1868.[8]

Buffalo and Niagara Falls were *last stops* on the Underground Railroad. It was not uncommon for Southerners visiting the American side of the falls to bring their slave house servants along with them. Area free African Americans worked hard at spiriting these folks across the river to Canada and freedom, a practice that infuriated tourists from southern states.

Susan B. Anthony, the women's suffrage leader, was instrumental in attracting Frederick Douglass, his wife, and their four children to make their home in Rochester, New York, in 1847. Mr. Douglass was an ex-slave who became a famous abolitionist, publisher, and lecturer about the evils of slavery. It should be noted that in 1858, *John Brown* stayed at the Douglas home while planning ways to encourage a slave revolt. During the Civil War, Douglas was also an adviser to *Abraham Lincoln* on the subjects of slavery and how African Americans should be granted citizen rights, such as voting, after the war. [9]

Reuben E. Fenton (1819-1885) emerged from the Kiantone area in the 1850s to serve as a state and national political leader. From 1846 to 1852 he served as *Supervisor of the Town of Carroll*, which at time included the area that became the Town of Kiantone in 1853. Fenton served in the *United States House of Representatives* from 1853 to 1855. A dedicated abolitionist, the very first speech he made on the floor of the House was in support of repealing the *Missouri Compromise*, also known as the *Compromise of 1850*.

The Missouri Compromise made it illegal for any citizen to aid a runaway slave. It also mandated that each citizen was required to report any sighting of runaway slaves and turn them over to federal authorities for deportation back to their owner. Citizens who ignored these guidelines were subject to a hefty $1,000 fine and possible imprisonment.

A disturbing example of how the Missouri Compromise was enforced took place in nearby *Busti, NY* (Map 1) on October 3, 1851 and is well-documented in the late Grace Fosberg's paper, "The William Storum Family: About the Facts and Incidences Pertaining to One of the Three Most Prominent Abolitionist Families in the Town of Busti". A runaway slave had taken refuge on the *Storum farm*, owned by free African Americans. He was spotted by slave chasers and taken into custody. The slave chasers hastily proceeded to Jamestown with the goal of taking a train to Buffalo. There they planned to appear before the Federal magistrate who would give them the necessary documentation for returning the slave to his Southern owner.

A rescue attempt was quickly launched by local abolitionists. By pre-arranged signal, farm and church bells were rung around Busti and, thus alerted, local townspeople, intent on rescuing the man, took off after the slave catchers. Alas, the local initiative failed and the man was returned to the South where he remained a slave until Lincoln's *Emancipation Proclamation* in 1862 set the stage for his eventual freedom in 1863.

Interestingly, Congressman Fenton, who would later serve as *Governor of New York State* from 1865 to 1869 and a *United States Senator* from 1869 to 1875, was not anti-slavery in the broad sense of the term. Rather, he was against the spread of slavery from Southern states to United States territories, a political middle-of-the-road position also held by Abraham Lincoln during most of his political career. Straddling the political center, Fenton first left the *Democratic Party*, which was pro-slavery, and then helped form the *Republican Party*. The result was that he lost his House seat for a term, but then was re-elected to it and served in the House from 1857 to 1865.

Evidently, Fenton's political position on slavery made him ultimately electable by the citizenry who concurred with his views. This was confirmed in 1860, when Chautauqua County voted by a two-thirds majority in favor of Abraham Lincoln. These votes represented many people in the northern sector of the nation, some of whom deplored slavery, but deplored division within the nation even more. The feeble hope, which proved to be futile, was that people like Fenton and Lincoln could preserve the Union without allowing slavery to spread. Alas, the Union eventually was preserved, but at the horrific cost of the Civil War. Slavery was ended in the United States, with its elimination only a by-product of the terrible struggle to preserve the Union.

Against this theological, social, and political backdrop which existed locally, regionally, and nationally, Kiantone citizens were faced with making personal decisions about how they would react to the issue of slavery. Some most likely opened their homes to the UGRR, helping runaway slaves as they made their way to well-documented UGR stations, such as the *Thayer Farm* on the Frewsburg-Kennedy Road and other sites in Jamestown. Others, out of fear of reprisal or simple lack of courage, probably shied away from such activity. However, the issue of slavery would not go away quietly or simply. The time was fast approaching when slavery would seize the entire nation, including Kiantone, in its immoral and reprehensible chains.

CHAPTER 5

RAPPING AND TUNNELING

THE MID-1800's SPIRITUAL CLIMATE

By 1850, the *United Brethren* denomination began to organize congregations in the Jamestown area. Thus, these German-speaking Methodists added their particular version of *Mainline Christianity* to the work of the *Methodist Episcopal, Presbyterian, Congregationalist, Baptist,* and other congregations who were already active in the Kiantone region.

However, these denominations did not have a lock-hold on the minds and souls of all persons. Spiritual fires were being kindled in ways that seemed to some folks as radical, suspicious, and even dangerous. Others looked upon the new spiritual practices as hope-giving and life-transforming.

Extraordinary and often unusual spiritual fires burned in Western New York for several decades in the 1800s. During this time, various "spirited religions, reform movements, sectarian groups, and a few cults",[10] eventually caused the area to be dubbed by one writer as the "Burned-over District".[11] A friend in Indiana once asked me why this was so. Others have asked the same question, most recently and most notably Susan Briand Morrow in her book, *Wolves and Honey: A Hidden History of the Natural World.* Unfortunately, though Morrow eloquently asks the question, she never really gives an explicit answer. The only explanation I could give my friend was my hunch that there is something about Upstate and Western New York's[12] breath-taking geography and seasons, which are both lovely and extreme, that made people expansive in their theological thoughts and reflections.

The area, of course, prior to the opening of the lands west of the Alleghenies to White Anglo settlers, was the frontier of early America. It is bounded on two sides by *Lake Erie*, the shallowest of the Great Lakes, and *Lake Ontario*, the smallest, but, also, the second-deepest. Connecting these two bodies of water is the thirty-three mile long *Niagara River*, including its seven-mile gorge and the whirlpool rapids, and the splendor of *Niagara Falls*. The area also is home to such unusual geographic features as the famous glacial *Finger Lakes*, scenic *Letchworth Gorge* on the *Genesee River*, the unusually deep and narrow *Watkins Glen*, prehistoric rock out-croppings such as *Olean Rock City* and *Panama Rocks*, and, in addition to the Niagara and Genesee rivers, the Allegheny River. It is, indeed, a beautiful area with deep winter snows, splendid springs, typically gentle summers, and autumns awash in brilliant colors. That is the only explanation I can give regarding why Western New York was the breeding ground for so many religious innovations in the early 19th Century. I am not sure it is the right answer, nor sure that there is, indeed, any correct answer. Such is the nature of theological mysteries.

Whatever the cause, Upstate and Western New York saw an abundance of religious innovations in the late 18th Century and early to mid-19th Century. In 1790, *Jemima Wilkinson*, from Rhode Island, a former Quaker woman also known as *The Publick Universal Friend*, joined members of her sect in Western New York. They were seeking freedom from persecution by orthodox Christians in New England. They first settled near *Seneca Lake* and then moved to another site a few miles west of *Crooked* (now *Keuka*) *Lake*. There Jemima led her followers, who believed she would be resurrected from the dead and proclaimed a messiah. The sect died out after she died (and presumably stayed dead!) in 1819.

It should be noted that the *Second Great Awakening* was making itself known during this time. Spanning a period from the late 1790s to the 1840s, this Protestant revolution saw the rise of great revival meetings, outdoor church camp meetings, and great membership growth, particularly among Methodists and Baptists. Marked by a high level of emotionalism, the Second Great Awakening was viewed by some congregations and clergy, particularly among Presbyterians, Congregationalists, and Episcopalians, as inappropriate and sensational.

In addition to high levels of Methodist and Baptist activity, the Second Great Awakening triggered other religious movements. From a 21st Century viewpoint, it is disturbing to read accounts of *The Kingdom of Matthias*, another sect that sprang up in the early 1830s with activities centered around *Harlem* and *Sing Sing*, NY. Paul E. Johnson and Sean Wilentz offer a remarkable look at this unsettling religious group in their book, *The Kingdom of Matthias: The Story of Sex and Salvation in 19th Century America*. Matthias, born *Robert Smith*, was a self-styled prophet who railed against a variety of people including clergy, Jews and women. Although he eventually lost his followers due to religious fantasies, sexual degeneracy, and alleged murder, it is said that Matthias made his way west as a self-proclaimed missionary of his beliefs. He died in 1841, and his theological message died with him. This story is all the more strange because one of his faithful followers was an ex-slave named *Isabella Van Wagenen*. She later took the name, *Sojourner Truth*, and became one of America's leading women in the Abolitionist Movement.

Perhaps one of the most familiar groups that sprung up during the mid-1800s was *The Church of Jesus Christ of Latter Day Saints*, or

Mormons, as they are commonly called. The founder of this group was *Joseph Smith,* also a product of the Second Great Awakening. Smith became discontent with orthodox Christianity. He claimed to have found additional Christian scriptural writings in a hill outside *Palmyra, NY,* a town located on the east side of Rochester. The practice of *polygamy,* whereby a man was married to more than one wife at a time, eventually drove the Mormons to Utah where some Mormon breakaway sects still practice polygamy today.

The *Shakers* found converts in Upstate New York during the early 1800s and invited them to join their communitarian societies. They were known for their functional and high quality products and designs as well as their practice of shaking their bodies to rid themselves of evil spirits.

The *Oneida Community,* another communitarian group, was founded by *John Humphrey Noyes* in the 1840s. They espoused beliefs that Christ had already returned to earth and that believers attained sinless perfection at the moment of Christian conversion. In addition to these unorthodox beliefs, the Oneida Community also held to practices such as *complex marriage,* an arrangement by which every male in the community was married to every female, who, likewise, was considered to be married to every male. Far from being licentious, this practice provided for a strict code of sexual behavior among its members known as *male continence.*[13] Suffice it to say that older men introduced young women to sexual activity, older women introduced young men to the same, and that is all that I am going to explain in this book about this unusual practice! Inquiring minds will have to do their own research to learn more.

Even in more orthodox circles, the mid-19th Century saw spiritual innovations. Outside of Rochester in the 1850s, *The Reverend B.T. Roberts,* a Methodist Episcopal clergyman, and his followers, known as the *Nazarites*, practiced a renewed form of Methodism that took a strong stand against slavery and membership in secret societies. In addition, the Nazarites also declared that all of its church pews were to be *free*, that is, not subject to family rental fees and they also instituted strict behavioral standards for church members. The Nazarites affirmed the *holiness movement*, an extension of John Wesley's *doctrine of perfection* that urged believers to seek, first, the forgiveness of sins and, second, the removal of human flaws that caused sin.

Roberts' beliefs resulted in his being expelled by the Methodist Episcopal Church. He and his followers then formed the *Free Methodist* denomination in 1860. This may, by 21st Century standards, sound like tame stuff. However, I once served as pastor of the *Spencerport United Methodist Church*, located a few miles west of Rochester. This congregation has in its possession a hand-written account of the church's history from the 1850s. It makes reference to the Free Methodist split from the Methodist Episcopal Church by simply saying that it was all so radical and difficult that the person writing the history simply could not and would not commit the details to the written record.

The spiritual fires of many mid-19th Century people also began to find their orientation in the *culture of death* that pervaded their time in history. This sounds maudlin, but actually it was not. During this time, many people came to view death as a difficult transition, but something more natural than previously thought. The *Rural Cemetery Movement* emerged, a major cultural shift that involved placing new cemeteries in the countryside, rather than in church courtyards. Part of the reason for this shift was the attempt to remove death from the sphere of organized religion. This was a reaction to the extreme revivalism that had made contemplation of death, especially for those not considered to be saved Christians, a morbid reflection full of the horrors of an eternal, fiery, punishing hell.

Despite philosophical reflections on the holistic nature of death, people in the 19th Century *continued to die*, often in large numbers! Infant mortality rates remained high. Death was far more apt to occur at a younger age. Twenty percent of all infants died before the age of one year. The average adult life expectancy was 48. Epidemics, such as the 1832 and 1849 cholera epidemics, swept away entire families almost overnight. Out of such suffering sprang a pathos that reached its full impact in the horrific deaths of the Civil War. Gary Wills poignantly and comprehensively explains these realities in his book, *Lincoln at Gettysburg: The Words that Remade America*, describing in detail the culture of death that accompanied Lincoln's consecration of that great burial field.

Many 19th Century people experienced a crisis of faith as they struggled with the unfolding culture of death. This crisis caused them to abandon traditional faiths, such as Christianity and Judaism, that were rooted in more historical and orthodox belief systems. They turned, instead, to *Spiritualism*, a new expression of faith, containing some aspects of Christianity and Judaism, that focused on talking with the dead.

The roots of Spiritualism are found in the writings of the 18th Century philosopher, *Emanuel Swedenborg*, who wrote of talking with the spirits of the deceased, God, Jesus and even the angels. In the early 19th Century, *Andrew Jackson Davis*, known as *The Poughkeepsie Seer*, went on the lecture circuit saying that he had had visions of Swedenborg. Davis eventually came to be known as the *Father of the Modern Spiritualist Movement* as well as "one of America's foremost writers on paranormal, occult, and 'psychic' powers."[14]

From a historical perspective, the public awareness of Swedenborg's writings and Davis's lectures, together with a fast-developing culture of death, may have set the scene for what was about to happen in *Hydesville, NY*. Or, maybe not. Again, it is difficult, if not impossible, to explain a mystery. Nevertheless, in a village lying about 32 miles east of Rochester, two girls were about to make paranormal history. In 1848, two young sisters, *Kate and Maggie Fox*, began to hear strange thumping sounds, often described as *rappings*, in the night. The sisters developed a decoding system for these raps, and said they were messages from deceased persons' spirits. Support for the Fox sisters' revelations came from words Andrew Jackson Davis understood that God had spoken to him on March 31, 1848, "Brother, the good work has begun. Behold, a living demonstration is born." Although the Fox family had heard the noises from the time they moved into the house in late 1847, it is curious that the public became aware of what was happening to Katie and Maggie at approximately the same time that God spoke to Davis.

The story of the Fox sisters has been told in many printed sources, including the recent *New York Times* bestseller, *Talking to the Dead: Kate and Maggie Fox and the Rise of Spiritualism* by Barbara Weisberg. The Fox sisters had a ready made audience in the 19th Century culture of death. For those who flocked to the Fox sisters for séances, Spiritualism represented a way of saying that their loved ones could still be counted upon for communication, for hope, and for encouragement. As noted previously, in the Second Great Awakening, preachers zealously proclaimed the prospect of eternal suffering in Hell for non-believers. Through Spiritualism, loved ones sought information regarding their deceased family and friends' ultimate destinies.

It should also be noted that the sisters' father, *John Fox*, was a devout and pious Methodist Episcopal and remained a faithful member of this denomination throughout his life. In 1726, *John Wesley*, the *Founder of Methodism*, wrote that his father's house had a ghostly spirit that the family called, *Old Jeffrey*. John Wesley was not living at home during this time, but there are several letters between Wesley and his mother documenting this strange occurrence. Wesley seemed to think that ghosts and spirits were one way to prove the supernatural nature of faith, while his mother, *Susannah Wesley*, was more inclined to think such matters were the providence of God and not for human understanding. Information was published about the family's ghost in 1823, in a work entitled, *Memoirs of the Wesley Family*. So popular was the book that another edition of it was published in the 1840s. Many Methodist Episcopal folks were quite taken with the book and conversations about it abounded in their fellowship. Thus, some of these persons, perhaps including some members of the Fox famnily, found it easy to make the jump from Methodism to Spiritualism.

By the early 1850s, many Americans were swept up in the notion of *talking to the dead*. News of the activity spread quite rapidly over the entire New York State landscape as well as to neighboring states. It is not surprising, therefore, that another Spiritualist chapter was about to unfold along the Kiantone Creek.

Early settlers, as noted in Chapter 2, were aware that Chief Cornplanter had taken the sick and infirm to the Kiantone Springs for healing. Early on, the springs caught the imagination of local settlers. In fact, they became known by a variety of names: *Lost Waters of the Magnetic Springs*, *Deer Lick Springs*, *Sulfur Springs* (because of the water's slight taste of sulfur), *Kiantone Springs*, and *The Romantic Kiantone Springs* (my personal favorite!).

Some of the springs belonged to a *John Chase*, a blacksmith living in Pennsylvania just across the border from Kiantone. There are both primary and secondary resources noting that in 1850 (some sources say 1853), his wife and daughter engaged in a Kate-and-Maggie-Fox-type trance. Genealogy records, however, point to John Chase and his wife, but offer no helpful clue regarding the presence of a daughter at that time. While in the trance, they learned of *web-footed Celtic Indians* who, according to the women, were buried deep under the springs. When I told one of my Indiana friends about this, she responded with a dumbfound look on her face, and asked, "You mean Indians wearing kilts?" The only answer I could give her was "not exactly, but close".

It should be noted that this was not Mrs. Chase's first encounter with the spiritual realm. In or about the year 1838, Mrs. Chase had visited a fortune teller in a neighboring town. The fortune-teller told Mrs. Chase that, in her absence, her husband had purchased a piece of land in the Kiantone Valley that contained a hidden treasure. Mrs. Chase scoffed at the idea, but, much to her surprise, learned upon returning home that her husband had, indeed, purchased the property as described by the fortune teller. The property was purchased to be used in a wagon construction business with another man, but the joint venture never materialized. There is no record as to whether Mrs. Chasse continued to seek direction from fortune-tellers during the ensuing years.

Regarding the Celtic Indians, Mrs. Chase and her daughter reported that while they were in the trance, they saw some kind of *hieroglyphics* that communicated the story about the web-footed Celtic Indians. The women understood the Celtic Indians to be spirits that were trapped in the earth under the springs. These people, according to Mrs. Chase and her daughter, had lived centuries before Columbus arrived in America in 1492, and had, at one time, been a refined and highly cultivated society. They had no system of law or government, but, rather, were ruled by the impulses of their own pure and holy hearts. The Celtic Indians had only one law, the law of unrestrained free love. They had no marriage, which, according to the Chase women, supposedly made them a perfect society.

The Chase mother and daughter reported that the Celtic Indians were invaded by other civilizations. The invaders brought the institution of marriage with them, an institution that the Celtic Indians viewed as wicked. Eventually, to escape the other civilizations, the Celtic Indians were swallowed up by the earth, but not before they had concealed the springs.

Many historians and writers have had a good time making much fun and mockery of the Chase women's tales of Celtic Indians, thinking it just to be women's nonsense, just as my friend did. However, there is a bit of truth in what the women reported. Type *Celtic Indians* into an Internet search engine and you will find that several websites pop up quickly. Why? The answer is simple. Because the earliest pioneers to the American frontier were mostly men, they frequently took Native American wives and conceived children by them. Thus, we have significantly high numbers of Native American citizens today who can also lay claim to Celtic ancestry, that is, Irish, Scottish, Welsh, and various sources of British blood. The websites mentioned previously include photos of present day Celtic Indians at gatherings where they wear costumes that include both aspects of Native American traditional dress as well as, you guessed it, kilts!

That, of course, is interesting and perhaps somewhat amusing. But there is still more foundation to the Chase women's understanding of the Celtic Indians. The women spoke of learning about the Celtic Indians from some kind of hieroglyphics. The ancient Celts had no written language. However, when the Romans began to invade the British Isles a few hundred years after the birth of Christ, the Celts developed a rudimentary language based on the Roman alphabet. It used lines in varying lengths and configurations to represent letters. These were mostly used on gravestones and other markers.

The comparisons become stronger the more one delves into Celtic culture. The Celts had no formal government. Consider the following:

The Irish [Celts] gave the druids and druidesses, considered to be both wise and learned, the task of preserving information. They did this by committing to memory philosophical, natural, medical, legal, spiritual, political and military knowledge. For this reason they were sometimes called, "the hidden people," since their stored knowledge was hidden in the deep resources of their mind.[15]

As for having "pure and holy hearts", well, that was the very nature of the Celtic people prior to the Roman invasion. They were given the name "Celts", meaning, "strangers", by the Greeks. The Greeks encountered the Celts between 600 and 350 B.C., as the Celts migrated from their place of origin in present day northern Germany to the south, spreading both to Asia Minor as well as westward along the Mediterranean Sea and up the Atlantic Coast as far as Ireland. They were like "curious children, [and] often embraced new ideas and concepts with glee".[16] Not unlike Native Americans, the Celts saw the holiness in all things, humans, plants, and animals and the very world around them. Men and women were considered equals in Celtic culture and, interestingly, both served as warriors in times of war. They highly valued children, including infants, and took good care of their older and sick relatives.

Like the Celtic Indians in the Chase women's trance, the Celts were eventually conquered, first by the Romans, then the Vikings and then by England. As far as disappearing down into the earth, well that would be, for the Celts, who saw goodness in all things, as good a place to hide as any. And, evolution aside, if you are going to live under a spring, web feet would be an advantage.

The Chase trance was the root beginning of Spiritualism as practiced at Kiantone. It is very likely that, by 1850, the Chase women had heard of the Fox sister's *rappings*, so it cannot be said whether or not they would have had these experiences if they had not heard of what was happening in Hydesville, some 180 miles away. John Chase was part of the family that helped to establish the Universalist Church of Kiantone and it is true that a few Universalists were quick to embrace Spiritualism. He formed a partnership with another neighbor, Spiritualist *William Brittingham*, and lost no time in seeing the incredible tales of the women as a way to profit. This, of course, sounds a bit mercenary. My hunch, however, is that Chase and his family were probably struggling financially and, thus, it is too harsh to say that he was only interested in financial reward. Rather, if Spiritualism and web-footed Celtic Indians put bread on the table, then so be it.

At this point, I am compelled to state that there is not a clear historical trail regarding what happened next. Various historical documents from the period are sarcastic in nature, while later histories take vast liberties with their interpretation of the truth. The researcher, myself included, is thus forced to piecemeal together the saga of these supposedly unusual springs.

Chase and Brittingham started digging and soon unearthed the springs, which they promptly dubbed the *Magnetic Springs*. The men determined, although there was no scientific basis to their findings, that the springs had a magnetic, as in both positive and negative, therapeutic characteristic. They sent water samples to various other Spiritualists for analysis. Meanwhile, Brittingham and Chase boiled down the water in large sap kettles to produce a salve. It was reported that, when the boiling process became too slow, they, or Chase's sons, added blue clay from the stream banks to boil it down faster. The resulting product was called, *A Spiritual Cure for All*. Chase and Brittingham advertised the salve in a Buffalo newspaper, stating that one did not even need to come to the springs for healing. According to them, one needed only to send a lock of hair or a handwriting sample of a sick person, plus two dollars, and the salve would be sent to the purchaser including a diagnosis based on the hair or handwriting.

Well, it may have been the water, but the sulfurous fluid emitting from the spring certainly had a whiff of snake oil about it! In time, Chase and Brittingham built a large house containing some 35 rooms which they dubbed, *The Castle*, for visitors who wished to experience the Magnetic Springs themselves. Actually, few people made the trip to Kiantone because the location, at that time, was still quite remote. The hotel venture was a flop and local folks eventually called it, *Brittingham's Folly*.

Word of the wondrous powers of the Magnetic Springs spread throughout the region. In late summer of 1853, more Spiritualists from the *Cleveland, OH* area came to Kiantone. Working with Chase and Brittingham, they helped dig a relatively large tunnel in search of treasure that was supposedly buried with the Celtic Indians. A tunnel 227 feet long (other sources say it was 270 feet long) was dug into the side of the hill. Reportedly, it was large enough for two persons to walk in it side by side, lined with timbers, six feet high, and set into the steep hillside at a forty-five degree angle. Alas, no treasure and no Celtic Indians were found. The tunnel eventually filled with water and had to be abandoned, its entrance boarded up so no one could enter it.

My head swam while writing this chapter. So many religious experiments, so many competing philosophies and spiritualities! And yet, that was precisely the spiritual landscape that Upstate and Western New York citizens experienced in the late 1700s and much of the 1800s. One of the hallmarks of the new American nation was freedom of religion and folks were engaging in that freedom with all the cultural background, ethnic diversity, spiritual creativeness, and orthodox piety that they could summon to mind and heart.

And so, we are left with the Chase mother and daughter's revelations about Kiantone's mythic Celtic Indians. It is possible that they might have had access to information about historic Celtic culture through a wandering scholar or rare book that might have found its way to them. Mrs. Chase could have learned of the Celts via an older relative who had committed Celtic history to memory. They may actually had known personally, or known of someone near their community, who considered him or herself to be a Celtic Indian.

Or, maybe, they actually did talk to the dead.

CHAPTER 6

John Murray Spear

Brilliant Social Reformer,
Head Injury Victim,
Or Both?

Plowing through hand-written documents from the 1850s and 1860s is no easy task. I found the work bogging me down, especially since my eyesight is less than perfect. Eventually, I contracted with a young *Purdue University* student to transcribe several of the documents for me. It was a challenge, but this brilliant soon-to-be sophomore slugged through the job and presented me with hard copies and a CD-Rom of her work.

When she brought them to my home, I could sense that she was pleased with her accomplishment. I was curious to know what she thought about the subject matter. Knowing she loves mysteries, science fiction, and fantasy literature, I just had to ask her what she thought of *John Murray Spear,* leader of a group of social reformers and Spiritualists who came to Kiantone in the early 1850s. My young friend did not miss a beat in answering the question. "He was insane!" she emphatically replied, seemingly glad that I asked the question so she could get her evaluation of this unique man off her chest.

Strangely enough, I think John Murray Spear would not have been surprised by her response and perhaps would have chuckled a bit about it. In his autobiography, *Twenty Years Under the Wing: Brief Narrative of My Travels and Labors as a Missionary Sent Forth and Sustained by the Association of Beneficents in Spirit Land,* Spear acknowledged those who had a low opinion of him and his work.

> *Very few have so understood my mission that they could give me either counsel or assistance, and therefore my trust has been in the invisible world.. Most persons have doubted if the spirits from whom I claimed to have received my commission, had even an existence, and not a few considered me deluded, if not demented, when I assured them it was my belief that they did exist, did communicate, and had organized to promote certain specified purposes.*[17]

Spear wrote this short autobiography, a pamphlet really, 20 years after coming to Kiantone. By his own veiled admission, it was as much a fund-raising tool as a record of his work. *Allen Putnam,* a Spear supporter who wrote the pamphlet's preface in October 1872, was bolder in writing about the purpose of the autobiography. He clearly stated the hope that those who read it, particularly those to whom Spears had been of some assistance, would "give some substantial tokens of their personal regards."[18]

But I am getting ahead of this story and the historical account of this seemingly insane man. As noted in the previous chapter, a group of Spiritualists came to Kiantone from Cleveland to investigate the reported healing benefits of the springs. The most illustrious of these visitors was a Spiritualist who had just recently become a medium, John Murray Spear (1804-1887). Spear believed that he was called to be a *missionary medium,* that is, one called by the spirits to be sent to others who needed his ministry, particularly those in need of some kind of healing. He was a unique, if not eccentric, person who was known by many strange monikers and descriptions, including the report that he caught fish "Dowie-like".[19]

John Murray Spear was born in Boston, MA, to a family who were members of the Universalist denomination. *Universalism* was established in the 1770s in New England. It is a fairly liberal denomination, combining both genuine faith and social action. The Universalists joined with the Unitarians in 1961 to form, as one of my friends calls it, the "UU's".[20]

Spear was born into a relatively new denomination still full of the energy imparted by its original members. He was, in fact, baptized by none other than *John Murray*, the *Founder of Universalism*, and named after him. In answer to the question, "What's in a name?" the answer can only be "a lot" if you have that kind of heritage. My great aunt was Flora Wyman Kidder, husband of Samuel Kidder. Together they founded *Kidder Memorial United Brethren* (now United Methodist) *Church* in Jamestown, NY with some assistance from my paternal great-grandmother on my mother's side. That family heritage has more than once fueled my spiritual fires when they were in danger of going out. There is no doubt that John Murray Spear, in his early years, sought to honor the man whose name he bore.

Spear, as a young man, spent some time apprenticed to a shoemaker, but that career was not to last. As a young adult, he studied for the Universalist ministry in Roxbury, MA. During that time he lived in the home of *Hosea Ballou*. This was heady stuff, since Hosea Ballou was "the most influential of the preachers in the second generation of the Universalist movement".[21] Again, this is very heady stuff, very heady, indeed! A person, especially a young, sensitive man like John Murray Spear, could easily begin to develop a vision of loftier aspirations surrounded by The Revered John Murray and Hosea Ballou, or any noted theologian or preacher.

Spear preached his first Universalist sermon in 1828 at *Barnstable (Hyannis), MA*. He was ordained and installed by that congregation in 1830 and subsequently served Universalist societies at *New Bedford, MA* (1835-1841) and *Weymouth, MA* (1841-1845). Note that these were fairly lengthy pastorates which, no doubt, gave Spear the opportunity to become well known to his congregations and establish good ties with them. He also continued during this time to network with distinguished Universalist leaders and other notable people.

In 1844, John heard *William Lloyd Garrison* (1805-1879) speak about the evils of slavery. Garrison was a passionate abolitionist who many historians consider to be the most radical of that group. He advocated, not for freeing the slaves and sending them back to Africa, as many seemingly well-intentioned folks desired, but, rather, for granting freed slaves full rights as American citizens.

John Murray Spear, a man always concerned with the plight of the less fortunate, soon became an outspoken abolitionist. His decision to join the Abolitionist Movement cost him his pastorate. He also lost his friends who were not yet ready to support what was, by that day's standards, a radical movement.

Spear joined a group of abolitionist speakers, including Frederick Douglass. He spoke frequently in 1844 across Massachusetts in an effort to spread the abolitionist sentiment and defeat the efforts to send slaves back to Africa. At a lecture in *Portland, ME*, Spear was attacked by a mob who reacted violently to his abolition message. He received a serious head injury that required months of healing and rest. One wonders if that clunk on the head did not contribute to shaping his future. The reality is that after the Portland incident, Spear displayed tendencies towards brilliant social reform coupled with, well, as my young friend put it, seeming insanity.

Around this time, undeterred and filled with a fervent sense of compassion, Spear began a ministry on behalf of prison inmates, which he called a "mission of love".[22] He was not the first religious leader to minister to prisoners; he followed in the footsteps of another faith-based social reformer, *John Wesley*, the *Founder of Methodism,* and led the way for others, inluding *William Booth*, the *Founder of the Salvation Army.* From 1845-1847, Spear was part owner and co-editor in his brother Charles' newspaper, *The Prisoner's Friend.* During this time, Spear was instrumental in the creation of the *parole officer* as a concept designed to prevent recidivism among the prison population.

When the Fugitive Slave Law was passed in 1850, Spear became an active and vital operator on the Underground Railroad. He was also one of the organizers of the *Boston Vigilance Committee*, another group that assisted slaves in their flight to freedom. Throughout this time, Spear ministered to some of the nation's neediest people. Surely, this drained his physical, emotional, and even his spiritual strength. Part of the reason he was able to continue with this difficult work was the personal counsel and assistance he received from notable persons including *Henry W. Longfellow (1807-1882)*, the renowned American poet, and *Horace Mann (1796-1859)*, considered by many to be the *Father of American Public Education.* It should also be noted that Spear was not employed by a Unitarian congregation during the years following 1845. During this time, he must have become somewhat of an accomplished fund-raiser, something he was forced to do in order to survive. His fund-raising skills would serve him well in the next chapter of his life.

John Murray Spear was seen by some as a mystic, by others a fanatic, and by still others as a visionary. Many historians and writers whose works I researched treated Spear with contempt, labeling him a charlatan, a cult leader, and other derogatory appellations. This is unfortunate. Spear was genuinely typical of a wide array of social and religious 19th Century *social reformers* who felt called to make right what was wrong in the United States and elsewhere. He lived in a time when the United States was still viewed by many as an experiment in democracy, a place where many sincere people were striving to create, if not a utopian reality, at least a better world. Their focus was on child education and labor, the workplace, people trapped in poverty, religious innovation, women's suffrage and the evils of slavery. They were not always right in their beliefs, but neither were they always wrong. Call them fanatics if you will, but they include some of our most distinguished citizens, such as *Harriet Tubman*, the heroic and tireless conductor on the Underground Railroad, and *Susan B. Anthony*, the temperance and women's suffrage leader. John Murray Spear was one of them and knew many of them personally. These reformers took the *Declaration of Independence*, the *Constitution*, and the *Bill of Rights* seriously. To some they appeared foolish, to others dangerous. They were a force to be reckoned with and could not and would not be ignored.

John Murray Spear was converted, though that may not be the best descriptive term, to Spiritualism on April 1 (no fooling!), 1852. He describes the actual event with scarce detail. However, he states quite clearly in his autobiographical pamphlet that the spirit messages he received at that time gave him specific details about how and when he should go to people in need of healing. Spear clearly believed that he was following the lead of his spirit directors by offering what he called "magnetic healing", a form of laying on of hands involving positive and negative polarities. He was, at least in part, encouraged in this work by his daughter, *Sophronia*, who had actually led Spear to Spiritualism.

On July 1, 1852, Spear began receiving a series of spirit messages from his namesake, the late John Murray. He recorded the messages in his own hand, but stated that it was Murray's spirit that caused his hand to write. These messages addressed "moral, religious, and spiritual"[23] issues. Spear again received two messages on September 11, 1852, which he this time dictated to his daughter, Sophronia. He did not include the text of these messages in his autobiography. The next day he received additional messages which he recorded in his own hand.

The messages received on September 12, 1852, presented an outline of the duties Spear was asked to accomplish. These included an announcement that Spear would heretofore be directed in his work by a band of "spirit friends".[24] The document appeared to communicate that Spear, with the assistance of his new spirit world buddies, would be addressing a wide range of social issues. These included the abolition of slavery, promotion of brotherly love, and the decrease of crime. Spear was undoubtedly comforted by their assuring message of support, "... your wants will be supplied as they come unto you".[25] The spirit friends were named as:

Benjamin Rush	*John Spear*
Oliver Dennett	*Franklin*[26]
Thos. [sic] Jefferson	*Zacheus Hamlin*
John Howard	*Joseph Hallett*
John Murray	

Still, at this time, as Spear noted in his autobiography, he was somewhat unsure about the validity of Spiritualism. He soon had the opportunity to hear a speech in Roxbury, MA about Spiritualism given by the aforementioned Allen Putnam. That speech and the social class rank and respectability of those gathered convinced Spear of the worth of this new spiritual avenue.[27]

Spear wrote that he continued to receive messages throughout the coming months. Once again, he cites no record of the content of these messages. And then, on April 1, 1853, just one year to the day after his first Spiritualist experience, Spear received a very special message from an *Association of Beneficents*, a group of spirit formed persons (*i.e.*, dead people), who told him that he was to serve as their earthly scribe. They communicated through Spear that they had banded together in the afterworld, or *Summerland*, as Spiritualists call it, and were now trying to communicate to the world of the living through him. They were listed as:

Benjamin Rush	*Roger Sherman*
Joseph Hallet	*Thos. Jefferson*
Benjamin Franklin	*Oliver Dennett*
John Murray	*John Spear*
John Howard	*Thos. Clarkson*
John Pound	*I. T. Hoppner*

Upon receiving this message, John Murray Spear's life was virtually reshaped and redesigned. He was 49 years old, married with grown children and one child still at home, and a former ordained Universalist pastor recognized for his work on behalf of slaves and prisoners. His actions during the next 19 years would unravel everything he had accomplished to date. And he believed he was incapable of stopping this runaway chapter of his life because of his commitment to the Association of Benificents.

A truly fascinating paragraph in Spear's autobiography follows the association membership list:

It was now supposed I was insane. Physician and others were sent to converse with and examine me. I showed them the above commission. They looked upon me with tender, compassionate eye, and they decided that I had become a lunatic. I knew their verdict, and greatly worried that I might be confined in an asylum for the insane; but I was mercifully preserved from such unhappy fate. I was then made to avoid society, to write much, to make strange drawings, to do many things that I did not comprehend, and some that seemed to me quite foolish and ridiculous.[28]

Now, all of this, at least for purveyors of history, is simply good old rollicking entertainment to read today. But it is what came next in Spear's 1872 autobiography that is most surprising. Namely, Spear never mentioned the suspected mental illness again. Talk about denial! He just picked up with the tale of his life by saying that he traveled next to *Cleveland, OH*, 700 miles west of Boston. Did he go there to escape being sent to a mental asylum? Was he fleeing well-intentioned family members? Alas, we do not have answers to these questions and must content ourselves with his explanation that the spirits sent him to Cleveland.

While there, Spear met with like-minded Spiritualists. They arranged for him to make a public address in *Brainard's Hall*, a public place that offered music and theater productions. Spear had no idea what he was to say. But as he took the podium, a long speech emerged from his lips, purportedly on behalf of the Association of Benificents, in which he outlined their world reform platform. This platform was loosely organized into several categories, including *new things* such as a new era, new Church, new system of education, new governments and new garments. It also included other philosophical innovations arranged in trinities [*sic*, Spear's word]: *force, feeling, and wisdom* as well as *economy, convenience, and beauty* [italics added].[29] Of particular interest is the announcement that in the past, human activity had unfolded in an "angular" fashion, but now it would begin to be formed in *"circular understandings of truth* [*sic*, italics mine]".[30] This, like the Celtic Indians referred to previously, is a very Celtic notion, the circle being one of the main symbols of Celtic culture.

Spear delivered the speech while seemingly in a trance with his eyes closed. In his trance, he named a woman, *Caroline S. Lewis*, to be the "Leaderess".[31] He claimed he had no recollection of selecting her after the trance ended, nor did he see any specific role for her to play.

While in Cleveland, Spear felt called to visit some springs he had been told possessed certain special qualities. Bingo! The springs were located, as his document records, in *Farmington, PA*, right on the border with Kiantone, NY. They were, in fact, the same springs that belonged to John Chase, his brother *Oliver G. Chase*, and William H. Brittingham, but occupied only by John Chase and his family.[32] Spear recorded that he left for the springs on May 10, 1853, and that the purpose for the visit was as yet unknown to him, even after observing them, but he promised to visit them again soon. He then returned to Cleveland. Spear visited the Chase and Brittingham springs again on June 10, 1853, in the company of his daughter. He also indicated that on that visit, land was purchased by three of the Spiritualists accompanying him, *Horace Fenton, Dr. Abel Underhill*, and others in their company.[33] Although he does not mention it here in his autobiography, this land was not the land owned by Chase and Brittingham, but, rather, adjacent land to theirs that also had springs located on it. Spear referred to the land purchsed as, " . . . the domain where I now write (Kiantone) .

. . "[34] Note that the name, Kiantone, is indicated by Spear within parentheses. Obviously, he wanted his readers to know where he was writing his memoirs.

It is noteworthy that *Thaddeus S. Sheldon* wrote an essay in April 1853, stating that love is recognized as an element.[35] It should be noted that Sheldon's writing often reflected his knowledge of the work of Andrew Jackson Davis, indicating that he had surely either read or heard Davis' work. In this essay Sheldon included a list of persons that he believed to be genuine mediums, including John Murray Spear. According to Spear, he did not visit Kiantone Springs until May, but Sheldon, evidently, had at least heard of Spear by April 1853, when he wrote his essay.

At this point in the saga, we are left with the proverbial chicken or egg question. That is, we do not know if Kiantone was chosen as the site for Harmonia because of the availability of a seemingly significant Spiritualist medium, John Murray Spear, or if Spear was chosen because his mediumship was the perfect complement for the springs' mystical character. One possibility is that it was a bit of both. And remember, Spear needed a community, a group of patrons, to support him and his work. The Spiritualists, committed to Kiantone Springs and its development as a Spiritualist healing site, would provide that support.

At this time, Spear also made a trip, first to Rochester, NY, and then to Niagara Falls with Dr. Abel Underhill, the doctor who may have paid for this gallivanting around the Western New York area. Spear and another medium, *Charles Hammond*, announced in Rochester on June 30, 1853, that, in addition to the Association of Benificents, there were to be six additional associations in the spirit world:[36]

The Association of Electricizers

The Association of Elementizers

The Association of Educationizers

The Association of Healthfulizers

The Association of Agriculturalizers

The Association of Governmentizers

Note that the associations were to have a subordinate role to still another spirit world group, the *General Assembly*.[37] Spear's autobiography then continues with a transcription of another message from his spirit friends:

Something more than a year since, a number of persons in the spirit world resolved to associate together for the promotion of several scientific, useful, and philanthropic purposes. Organization was the result. A body called the GENERAL ASSEMBLY [sic, Spear's capitalization] was formed. Entering immediately on its duties, the General Assembly resolved to organize several subordinate bodies.[38]

Notice the use of the word, "since", in the above quotation. Did Spear mean "since" June 30, 1853, or did he mean June 30, 1854? Continuing to read the autobiography, we find that he most likely meant June 30, 1853, since this spirit message was immediately followed by the phrase, "While on my way back to my native city, from Rochester and the Falls. . ."[39] I offer the following list as my summary of this spirit message, which was loftily addressed to "THE INHABITANTS OF THIS EARTH [sic, Spear's capitalization]:

1. The spirits have recognized the need for an organizational body.

2. The Electricalizers, headed by Benjamin Franklin, is the most important of the associations.

3. The General Assembly is so named because those spirits who constitute it are of one mind.

4. The General Assembly will select earthly representatives, from the United States and elsewhere, who will support the work of the General Assembly.

5. The General Assembly has general plans including a new government, a new code of laws, and a new church.[40]

Subtly slipped into the last paragraph is a statement that some persons will be employed in this work. Thus, we see the financial implications which will underwrite Spear's missionary medium ministry.

The message is signed by *Daniel Webster* (1782-1852). He had not been mentioned previously, perhaps because he had only recently died. Webster was a statesman, lawyer, and orator from New Hampshire who served in the *United States Congress* and also as *Secretary of State*. What is specifically remarkable and relevant to his signing this spirit message was his role in the Missouri Compromise. This compromise (see Chapter 4) admitted California as a free state, but designated that newly acquired territories could choose whether to be slave or free states. It also included the Fugitive Slave Law. Webster's approval of the compromise was indicative of his overall concern that the Union be preserved and that the southern states not secede from it. What, then, does his signature here, on the spirit message Spear received, signify? A change of heart? A new revelation upon passing from the world of the living to the spirit world? Unfortunately, no answers to these questions were provided.

Immediately following was the list of earthly representatives, plus their places of residence, which Spear calls "the original twelve Teachers selected by the General Assembly":[41]

Adam Putnam, Roxbury Mass.,	Apostle of Precision
Johnathan Buffum, Lynn,	Distribution
Daniel Goddard, Chelsea,	Devotion
Eliza J. Kenney, Salem,	Government
Emily Rogers, Utica, N.Y.	Resignation
Thaddus S. Sheldon, Randolph, N.Y.	Harmony
Mary Garcner, Farmington, PA	Freedom
Angelina Mumm, Springfield, MA	Education
Eiliza W. Farnham, New York City	Direction
Jno. M. Sterling, Cleveland, O.,	Treasures
Thos. Richmond, Chicago, ILL.,	Commerce
George Haskell, Rockford,	Accumulation[42]

To this list Spear added the names of a few British citizens he selected for various positions. My personal favorite title is the "Celestial Poet", a role filled by Mary Howitt.[43]

Thus, equipped with his dead spirit friends, the seven associations of the spirit world, including the Association of Beneficents, the General Assembly, and his living Spiritualist friends, John Murray Spear secured his advisory council, his working committee, and his financial future. He also effectively announced sedition, a moral revolution, and a new church.

Only two of those activities were legal. The other was illegal. Or was it all just insanity caused by a clunk on the head?

CHAPTER 7

WHO WERE THESE PEOPLE?

THE LIVING SUPPORTERS
AND SPIRITUAL GUIDES

Who were these people? Why does it matter? While I was working on this book some of my Christian friends scoffed at these questions. Still others dismissed the questions as nonsensical, even spiritually dangerous to consider. Again and again, I found myself reminding my friends that I was writing a book from a historical perspective, not a faith perspective. Some were satisfied with that answer, while others simply told me that they were putting me on their prayer lists under the category of *endangered souls*.

In answer to the questions posed above, I can only answer that these persons, both living and physically dead, *mattered very much to John Murray Spear*. Spear and his living supporters were not perfect people, but they were men and women dedicated to a reform movement they believed would enhance, not denigrate, their society. Moreover, they mattered to each other. Finally, they believed Spear was receiving good counsel from the spirits of deceased persons who had led vital, transformational, and creative lives.

The famous and not-so-famous people who were named as John Murray Spear's spirit guides, the Association of Beneficents, and the General Assembly were intriguing to research. Spear must certainly have been thrilled to think that they had banded together in the afterlife, given their interests, abilities, talents, and experiences And, to think that they wanted to be *his* guides and *his* counselors, directing him in great cities as well as little old Kiantone, well, that had to thrill Spear even more!

Writing from a historically-based perspective, I first had to make some decisions about how I would research these folks. Obviously, since I am not a Spiritualist, contacting the physically dead through a medium was out of the question. So, I turned to that vast, mysterious, ethereal communication resource of my own time, the Internet. Various websites, most related to local historical societies, church groups, and educational institutions, supplied good information about the various historical persons. In addition, I also focused on those printed resources that could be considered as *primary*, including Spear's autobiography, the *Sheldon Papers*, and first-hand newspaper accounts.

I began by considering those earthly Spiritualist supporters without whom John Murray Spear would never have had the capital nor the assistance to proceed with the work he felt called to accomplish. He described these people as teachers who acted on behalf of the General Assembly. From his autobiography, I knew their names and the cities of their origin, but nothing else. Working with these two bits of information, I entered first their name and next their city into an Internet search engine, followed by a second entry that included each name plus the title, "spiritualist." I was amazed by what I found!

Adam Putnam, Jonathan Buffam, and *Daniel Goddard* were Spear's Spiritualist colleagues in the Boston area. Mr. Putnam was president of the *New England Spiritualists Association* that was organized in Boston in November, 1854. The teaching title given to Putnam, the *Apostle of Precision*, was possibly reflective of his organizational and leadership skills, given his presidency of that group. Daniel Goddard, that is, The Reverend Daniel Goddard,[44] was a vice-president of the same organization. I was unable to discover how he had acquired the clergy title, but my hunch is that he brought it with him from a Congregational, Unitarian, or Univeralist church. Daniel Goddard was deemed the *Apostle of Devotion*, probably because of his clergy status. Jonathan Buffum was called the *Apostle of Distribution* which probably meant that his role had something to do with competency in handling resources, given his election as Trustee of the New England Spiritualists Association.

Eliza J. Kenney, the *Apostle of Government*, showed up as a member of the 1854 *Massachusetts Spiritual Convention*[45] where she served as a member of the State Central Committee. This committee was entrusted with the work of planning a spiritualist national convocation in partnership with Spiritualists located in other states. This gives us some insight into Kenney's work as the Apostle of Government, indicating, perhaps, that she was skilled in organizational and implementation tasks. Spear was also listed in the aforementioned Massachusetts group as a member of the Business Committee, which makes for an interesting connection between Spear and Kenney.

I did not fare so well in researching *Emily Rogers*, the *Apostle of Resignation*, as I found no trace of her. Roger's responsibilities eluded me. Was she in charge of persons who wanted to resign from the Apostles? But why would that have been considered so early in the development of this group? Or was she in charge of some act of being resigned, as in the group cultivating a sense of accepting of the tasks they were to perform? One answer to that question might be the acceptance of their work as being guided by the General Assembly.

Thaddeus S. Sheldon (1818-1868), the *Apostle of Harmony*, was a delight to research. First, he was a local citizen, having moved in 1836, from Rupert, VT, to Randolph, NY, located about 19 miles east of Kiantone. Sheldon was an entrepreneur who became a prosperous general store owner and railroad developer. His entrepreneurial spirit was not limited to his own well-being. He became a community leader and one of the founders of the *Randolph Academy*. This was a higher education institution, but with a more frontier–like quality than what we usually think of as colleges and universities today. Sheldon was also one of the academy's best contributors. In addition, he shared his wealth with all churches and charities within his community. Captivated by a spirit of love, that is, the *agape* [Grk.], or universal form of love, Sheldon always extended love to friend and stranger alike. I think he was just a nice guy, even though, as we shall see, he developed some strange philosophies. It is interesting to note that Sheldon's biography located on the *Town of Randolph, Cattaraugus County Biography Project* website[46] makes no mention of his involvement with John Murray Spear, Kiantone, or Harmonia. This is a rather obvious omission. Sheldon's personal papers, including correspondence, essays, and reports about Harmonia, were discovered in a trunk by his granddaughter in 1941. They provide the basis for much of what we know about the Harmonia community and are now housed at the prestigious Darlington Memorial Library at the University of Pittsburgh. Omitting all this from the website noted above is curious, to say the least.

Mary Gardner, the *Apostle of Freedom*, lived in either Farmington, PA, a small settlement that abutted the Kiantone Springs site, or just across the border in Kiantone, NY, depending on various sources. It is possible that she initially lived in Farmington, but later records indicate that she eventually lived on the Harmonia property. She maintained both an interest in Harmonia as well as actual participation in the community from its inception to its demise and discontinuance. For example, a document dated January 1, 1861, in the *Sheldon Papers* outlines an agreement between Thaddeus Sheldon and Mary Gardner that "the Home department [*sic,* document uses lower case "c"] at Kiantone is to be under the sole authority of Mary Gardner, who will be known as the 'Matron of the Home Department'".[47] Her title, Apostle of Freedom, probably indicates involvement with the Underground Railroad.

Although it is easy to speculate about the meaning of her title, I found no clues as to the identity of *Angelina Mumm*, the *Apostle of Education*. The *Apostle of Direction, Eliza W. Farnham* (1815-1864), however, proved to have a fascinating biography. She was a novelist, feminist, and prison reform activist. Her best known novel was *Life in Prairie Land* (1846). Farnham was also a keynote speaker at the *1858 National Women's Rights Convention*. There was great and furious debate over the primary theme of her speech, namely, that women were superior to men.

Jno. [*sic,* John] *M. Sterling* of Cleveland, OH, shows up as a business and Spiritualist partner in the *Sheldon Papers*. Therefore, it is not surprising that he is the *Apostle of Treasures*.

No reference was found for *Thos.* [*sic,* Thomas] *Richmond*, Chicago, IL, the *Apostle of Commerce*. A Spiritualist named *Mary Richmond* surfaced in some of the research, but I could not determine if she was the wife, sister, or other female relative of Thomas Richmond.

George Haskell[48], *Rockford, IL,* the *Apostle of Accumulation*, showed up in a listing of Spiritualist magazines found in the 1856 *Spiritual Telegraph*, a directory of various mediums, lecturers, resources and achievements.[49] While perusing this resource, I had to chuckle that this publication's name was partly adapted from the newest communication technology of its day while I was using the newest communication technology of my own time. Anyway, in the *Spiritual Telegraph*, Haskell is listed as the co-editor of a Spiritualist magazine entitled, *THE NORTH-WESTERN ORIENT* [*sic*, resource cited uses capitalization]. That was the only resource I found listing a George Haskell who was a physician. However, it was not clear if he was the same George Haskell. But, it seems likely, given Spear's interest in healing plus the overall interest the Spiritualist movement had in healing. I also noted in the Illinois website that in 1855 he opened the *Haskell House* hotel in Rockford. I was curious about whether this was a hotel offering Spiritualists ministries, but found no reference to substantiate my hunch. Also, in Rockford today, there is a George B. Haskell Elementary School, but, again, that middle initial does not appear in other Spiritualist references, so it may well be a different George Haskell.

I have to admit that it was kind of exciting to research these folks! It was just plain fun! Pop in the name of one of Spear's cronies into a search engine, and bingo, there he or she was! Of course, I have done this before on the Internet. This time, however, was different. With great 21st Century technological ease, I was connecting the dots in a way that individuals who have previously written about Kiantone did not have at their disposal.

After checking out Spear's colleagues who were physically alive during his time, I turned to those persons whose spirits constituted the Association of Beneficents and the General Assembly, as well as the spirit friends who initially contacted Spear in 1852. As we have seen in the previous chapter, on September 12, 1852, Spear received information that he would be directed in his work by a band of spirit friends. When I first looked at the list of their names, I recognized some of them quickly. Others were unknown to me. Once again, I turned to the Internet and began to search their identity. This time I had only the persons' names to initiate the search. But, as before, I was amazed by what I found.

Benjamin Rush (1745-1813) was a signer of the Declaration of Independence. He was also "the most celebrated American physician and the leading social reformer of his time".[50] Rush's father was an Anglican, his mother was Roman Catholic, so he had a healthy dose of both, which may have had something to do with his becoming a Presbyterian. This eventually led him to becoming convinced of *universal salvation* and finding a spiritual home with the Universalists. More than simply being a member of that faith, Rush became a good friend of John Murray, the Founder of Unitarianism in America, and his wife, Judith.

Rush advocated for many social reform causes including prison and judicial reform, abolition of slavery, and the abolition of the death-penalty. He also supported education of women and conservation of natural resources. Moreover, Rush lobbied for the appointment of a *Secretary of Peace* to the federal cabinet and was appointed by President John Adams to serve as *Treasurer of the United States Mint*.

However, it was in the area of medicine and health that Rush saw his greatest success. He was an advocate for proper diet and abstinence from tobacco and alcohol. Although seemingly primitive by today's standards, Rush embraced blood-letting as an innovative way to treat disease. This was considered cutting edge medicine at the time. In 1786, he established the first free dispensary in the United States. Rush also advocated for preventive medicine, promoted inoculation and vaccination against smallpox, and pioneered in the study and treatment of mental illness, including the consideration of how people's dreams affect their mental well-being. For this work, he is known as the *Father of American Psychiatry*.

Oliver Dennett, unlike Rush, seems to have left no lasting legacy. The name shows up as a first name and middle name in the mid-late 1800s for a man who was a musician. The second reference I found was in the 1900s for an artist. There does not appear to be an Oliver Dennett who was a contemporary of John Murray Spear or someone who shared his interest in Spiritualism.

Thos. Jefferson[51] (1743-1825), of course, is a reference to Thomas Jefferson, the principal writer of the Declaration of Independence. While serving as the third President of the United States, Jefferson negotiated the purchase of the Louisiana Territory and facilitated the Lewis and Clark expedition. He held many other public offices including *Governor of Virginia, United States Minister to France,* and *Vice-President of the United States.*

Jefferson also advocated for the separation of church and state, also a central theme of the Universalist Church. He was an inventor and is remembered for developing what some call the *Jefferson Bible.* This work consisted of his cutting and pasting together various sections of the *New Testament Gospels,* particularly Jesus' teachings. These, according to Jefferson, most closely represented the overall philosophy of Jesus.

Jefferson maintained a strong anti-evangelical stance because he was a deist by faith. *Deism,* briefly, is the belief that God created the world, but does not seek to control it except as humans might obtain reason through contemplation of God's nature. Despite having been raised as an Anglican, Jefferson's beliefs were closest to the Unitarians, but he never formally joined that denomination. It is notable that Jefferson contributed money to every church near his home at *Monticello.*

Thomas Jefferson had deep moral reservations about the practice of slavery, but he never freed his own slaves. There has been much discussion about his relationship with *Sally Hemming,* a slave he owned, and the child they produced together. In modern times, the DNA of Hemming's heirs has been successfully linked to Jefferson.

John Howard (1706-1790) is considered to be the *Father of Prison Reform.* He was born in *Cardington, England.* During his lifetime, he became known as a sincere humanitarian, while also being a *Non-Conformist Christian.* That is, he joined the Congregationalists, Baptists, Methodists, Quakers, and Unitarians who sought to break away from the Anglican Church, also known as the *Church of England.* Howard's work included a systematic analysis of prison conditions in England, Europe, and Russia with reports about the filth, disease, torture, and death that he witnessed in those places. He did not advocate for prisoner issues such as eliminating the death penalty and encouraging rehabilitation. Instead, his work focused on creating a prison environment that was free from disease and filth.

John Murray, as noted in Chapter 6, was the Founder of the Universalist Church in America. He immigrated to America from *Gloucester, England,* in 1770 and subsequently founded the first Universalist Church in *Gloucester, MA.* Murray taught Universalism because he did not believe in the *Calvinist* doctrine of eternal punishment for unrepentant sinners. He coupled his Universalist beliefs with a strong commitment to ministering to impoverished and other needy persons.

Benjamin Franklin (1706-1790)[52] was a *Boston, MA,* printer and news-paper publisher. His most famous literary work was *Poor Richard's Almanac.* As a young man, Franklin became very civic-minded, working to establish public libraries, good sanitation, and fire fighters associations. He was an inventor and student of the new science of electricity. Franklin also was on the committee that drafted the Declaration of Independence. He subsequently wrote a very strongly worded anti-slavery document.

The only *Zaccheus Hamlin*[53] I found reference to was a man listed in a long genealogical study. Actually, the name appears as, *Zaccheus Hamlen*, but the surname also appears as Hamblin in the study. He was born June 17, 1711, in *Barnstable, MA* and married Mary Lomboard on July 29, 1736. Together they had 11 (or possibly 13) children. I found it interesting that there was no date given for Hamlin's death. Rather, there is just a notation that he was lost at sea. Pondering that, I realized that some sailors, sea merchants, and fishermen might just have left their families and towns to go elsewhere and start a new life. Still others may have been ship-wrecked and stranded far from home. Their families could never be sure if they were, indeed, lost at sea, stranded or had just taken off for a new life.

John Spear, most likely, was John Murray Spear's father. There is very little information about him available, aside from a record indicating that he married *Sally Corbet* on May 29, 1801. The Reverend John Murray performed the ceremony.[54]

Joseph Hallett's[55] story took a bit of digging, but was worth the effort. He was a British Presbyterian clergyman who held an *Arian* view of Jesus. This concept was named after the heretic, Arius, who believed that Jesus was neither fully divine nor fully human. Arianism pops up from time to time in Christian history, but it was labeled as a heresy by the *First Council of Nicaea* in 325 A.D. In 1717, Hallett was formally accused of Arianism because he was part of a group that would not subscribe to a creedal statement issued by the English Presbytery. Hallett and his group wrote a document explaining their resistance to the creed and that document is considered by Unitarians to be their *charter of dogmatic freedom*.

In turning from looking at Spear's spirit friends list to those who were revealed in September 1852, to be his Association of Beneficents, I noted that some were common to both lists and some were not. Those included on both lists were Benjamin Rush, Joseph Hallett, Benjamin Franklin (both first name and surname in second list), John Murray, John Howard, Thomas Jefferson, Oliver Dennett and John Spear. Those that were added to the Association of Beneficents list include John Pound, Roger Sherman, Thos. Clarkson, and I. T. Hoppner.

Once again, I turned to the Internet for information about the additional persons. Nothing was to be found about *John Pound* or *I. T. Hoppner*. However, Sherman and Clarkson were well documented.

Roger Sherman (1721-1793) was born in Massachusetts. He became a shoemaker to help support his family when his father died in 1741, but Sherman was destined for greater things. As a self-taught mathematician, astronomer, and lawyer, he passed the Connecticut bar and eventually became a judge in that state. He served as *Treasurer of Yale College* and was elected to the *Connecticut State Legislature*. Sherman was also a delegate to the *Continental Congress* where he helped frame the Declaration of Independence. His brilliant public service career included contributing to the writing of the Constitution and serving as a United States Senator from Connecticut. Sherman was reputed to be rooted in commonsense, possessing much integrity, and deeply pious.

Thomas Clarkson[56] (1760-1846) was a British abolitionist who recruited William Wilberforce to the cause. He was also an artist who documented the atrocities of slavery not with written reports, but by creating detailed sketches. His most famous drawing is one showing seized Africans packed so tightly into a slave ship that they could not stand up or move about. When the British *Slave Trade Act* was passed in 1807, *William Wordsworth*, the poet, honored Clarkson's role in securing passage of the legislation with these words,

CLARKSON! It was an obstinate hill to climb..

Thomas Clarkson also worked for the abolition of slavery both in England and world-wide.

Many common threads emerged when I reviewed the list of John Murray Spear's spirit friends, Association of Beneficents, and Apostles (teachers) who acted on behalf of the General Assembly. The Apostles, of course, shared Spear's commitment to Spiritualism. This is no small matter, given that this was a new spiritual movement. People in the early stages of such a group almost always have a non-extinguishable passion for the organization. Several were people of means, including Sheldon, Sterling, Haskell, and Farnsworth. Surely, Spear counted on them for substantial financial support. It is quite possible that some others in the group were also able to offer financial assistance.

Among the spirit friends list and the Association of Beneficients list there were also some similarities. Rush, Jefferson, and Franklin were noted statesmen who played large roles in the still relatively new United States of America. We think of them today as, perhaps, musty, old, historical forefathers, but keep in mind that each of them committed treason by signing the Declaration of Independence. Some of them fully expected to be hanged if the Colonists lost the Revolutionary War. These were men who lived life on the edge of a budding democracy that was as revolutionary as any other emerging government and social movement. In addition, each recognized that slavery was an unsettling factor in the new nation. To those three men, we can add Clarkson, whose work on behalf of eliminating both the slave trade and slavery itself, was cutting-edge in its day. There were several religious non-conformists in the group, including Murray, Rush, Howard,

Jefferson, Hallett, and Clarkson. But the *common thread* among all these men was that each, in some way, had used his life to promote social reform, including the abolition of slavery, and they were very successful in doing so. John Murray Spear had acquired just the kind of spiritual guide foundation he needed to achieve his own goals.

In conclusion, as the roots of Spear's emerging Spiritualist and social reform community were planted in Kiantone, two things were clear. First, John Murray Spear believed these physically dead, spirit-world people were guiding his every step and action. Second, he had amassed an articulate and powerful group of living persons to support and implement his work. Spear believed, with all his heart, that he had brought some of the most astute minds, both living and dead, to Kiantone and Harmonia Springs. He was convinced that together they would build a new world and make a positive and powerful contribution to society.

Some day powerful preachers, leaders, movers, and shakers would come to another splendid geographical site in Chautauqua County and make it famous. But it would not be Spear or his spirit friends, nor even his earthly friends. And, it would not be at Kiantone.

CHAPTER 8

THE HARMONIA HEYDAY
JUST WHAT WAS GOING ON?

Thaddeus S. Sheldon, on April 8, 1853, wrote an essay entitled, "There is a Law of Love."[57] Much has been written about John Murray Spear and his involvement with the Harmonia community, also known as the Domain.   However, there is ample evidence that one of the stronger, if not the strongest, nurturing personalities behind the community was Mr. Sheldon.

Sheldon states in his essay, "spiritualism is a philosophy of religion" and love is "an element in its own right".[58] These words, if they came from the pen of John Murray Spear, would not be surprising. However, coming from the pen of a risk-taking entrepreneur, they are, truly, words for thought.

There is a Law of Love. Records detailing the events that took place at Harmonia always reveal in the shadows and behind the scenes, not a controlling Rasputin-type mystic, nor a wizard in an emerald city, but, rather, this thoughtful businessman with a heart of love. This expression of love would play out in both mystical and, I dare say, erotic ways.

Thaddeus Sheldon was a business man, community leader, and education supporter. In many ways, his life was typical of his time. In 1839, he married *B. Rosetta Crowley*, but she died eight years later, possibly from childbirth, and left him with no children. Nine months later, although the timing does not appear to be significant, he married *Agnes E. Calhoun* and together they had several children. Other than his own papers, his obituary, and a Cattaraugus County genealogy website, there appears to be no other historical account of his family. One cannot help but wonder if either or both of Sheldon's wives, who may have been freethinkers themselves, somehow contributed to his seemingly strange and provocative philosophies. Of course, it is possible that by the time Sheldon married either wife he had begun to develop his unusual notions about marriage and family and was already seen as somewhat eccentric.

Sheldon eventually came to hold views that must have both-shocked and disturbed the residents of his rural hometown, Randolph, NY. John Murray Spear and others would come and go from Harmonia as the seasons of their hearts desired. However, Thaddeus Sheldon, despite his frequent business travels to New York City, Cincinnati, and other cities, always knew that his soul's delight, in addition to Randolph, was in the little spring-fed community on the banks of Kiantone Creek.

What then, took place at the *Domain* in Kiantone? The answer to that question depends on which sources one chooses to read and believe. Page after page about this community has been written by various historians, both amateur and professional. Some of these pages appear to be accurate and simply stated. Others are cloaked in layers of interpretation, according to the viewpoint of the writer as well as the literary style used, ranging from sarcastic to flowery Victorianism. And then, there are all those lengthy pages of séance transcriptions which some might choose to include in their research. As stated in the Preface, I mostly avoided the use of séance transcriptions, except for those that were directly related to actions taken by Spear and other members of his community.

My decision to base this book largely upon primary sources is clearly stated in the *Note about Sources*. However, even among these documents, there is not always agreement on dates, events, and persons. Thus, I found myself constantly checking back and forth among the records. In time, I realized that the accounts could be compared to four eyewitness describing one automobile accident, each having viewed it from a different street corner. That is, each writer had his or her own perspective and, perhaps, his or her own agenda, too.

Two of the most interesting eye-witnesses were *Mark Cheney* and *Wilbert Northrop*. Each spent time around the Domain when they were just young lads and Cheney actually worked for Spear's group. Records indicate they may have been eight to fourteen years old at the time. Years later, in old age, they were interviewed in 1924 by *William S. Bailey*, a local journalist. At the time of their interviews, their memories might have been a bit dim, but there was a boyish honesty about their reflections that remains both charming and informative.

Not quite primary documents, but not quite secondary in nature either, are works such as Emma Hardinge's, *Modern American Spiritualism: A Twenty Years' Record of the Communion Between Earth and the World of Spirits*. Mrs. Hardinge was neither a member of the Domain nor a resident of Kiantone. A Spiritualist and an incredible researcher, she worked diligently to document Spiritualism's early years even as they happened. Her work cannot be dismissed as merely a secondary resource. Works by Andrew Jackson Davis, sometimes called the *Father of American Spiritualism*, also fall into this category.

Still, it remained a challenge to sift through such works and distill from them the basic who, what, where, when, and why facts about what happened at the Domain. This is, frequently, a confusing story. Therefore, in preparing this book, it seemed most helpful to isolate each segment of the Harmonia story.

A Machine -

With a clearer description of the resources used in this chapter, we return to Spear's autobiography to see what happened next. Spear stated that he was in Rochester, New York on June 30, 1853.[59] He then made a reference to having received his extensive set of directives from the General Assembly "about a year after the commencement of these unfoldings".[60]

Spear then resumes his story again in 1853, stating that while on his way back from Rochester to Boston, he received new information, evidently some time after June 30, 1853.[61] This message from the spirit world revealed that he was to become involved with a machine, a perpetual motion machine, to be exact. For nine months thereafter, he received spirit messages about this machine. Spear described his involvement with it as follows:

> *They [the messages] came, and continued to come, for nine months: following out with precision the varied instructions as they were given, an external mechanism was elaborated, virbratory motion was secured, which was perpetual as long as the mechanism lasted; but on being removed by direction to Randolph, N.Y., a mob broke into the building in which it was stored, and the machine was demolished; though the principles brought out by its construction are preserved, and in due time that work, as I was informed, is to be resumed.[62]*

Oliver F. Chase, another local eyewitness to the Domain, lends further information about the machine. As with all of his observations about Harmonia, his witness is particularly helpful, since genealogical records seem to indicate that his father, Oliver G. Chase, was John Chase's brother.[63] Oliver F. Chase describes the machine as follows:

> *... a motor whose power, theoretically, was to be generated by the positive and negative magnetic and electric currents of the human body; the conception of a sort of "Electrical Walking Frankenstein." This machine met with hard usage at the hands of an unreasoning mob while at a house christened "Highrock Tower," built on a hilly suburb of Randolph, N.Y.*[64]

Chase is a bit confused here. *Highrock Tower* is mentioned in Emma Hardinge's book as being near Boston, MA where the machine was first constructed. It was subsequently moved to Randolph, a site in closer proximity to the magnetic qualities believed to be in that area. Chase's comments are helpful though, in that they confirm Spear's account. They also confirm that the machine was, indeed, destroyed by a mob in Randolph.

However, Chase's "Frankenstein" reference, a nod to *Mary Shelley's* 1818 novel, is not helpful. As we will see later, this is because Spear's ongoing interest in perpetual motion was generated, not out of a monster fascination, but, rather, out of his interest in labor reform. Specifically, Spear, by creating a perpetual motion machine, sought a way to ease the burden of the hard-working laborer. In this manner, he was like Shelley's character, *Dr. Frankenstein*, who created the creature in hopes of defeating disease and death.

Finally, it should be noted that Emma Hardinge's book and other sources give a long, lengthy description of a very peculiar event involving the supposed birth of the machine, that is, when it transformed from being a mere machine to becoming a living being. This, according to these sources, was accomplished by having a woman endure birth pains and, subsequently, engage in some mode of nursing the infant machine. All this took place in Massachusetts before the machine was moved to Randolph and it is simply too bizarre to consider with any sense of credibility. Moreover, unlike other aspects of the Harmonia story, it is not even amusing. It is just sick.

SPRINGS AND A TUNNEL –

With regard to the timing of events, involvement with the machine places Spear in Randolph some nine months after June 30, 1853, or about April 1854. Spear then wrote that he received messages telling him to go to Cincinnati, St. Louis "...and other important places",[65] where he gave numerous spirit-directed lectures. His narrative continued, "I was now instructed to again visit the *domain* [italics are Spear's] with some others, to engage in excavatory labors".[66] A description of the work follows:

> *It had been declared through several mediums that an ancient and highly cultivated people had dwelt there. Driven from this location, they here deposited certain valuables, which were to be exhumed and used for certain beneficent [sic, Spear's spelling] purposes. Here I worked, in the heat of summer and the frosts of winter, for seven months, entering into the bowels of the earth more than one hundred and thirty feet, enduring many privations, suffering much through doubt and anxiety of mind. When that work was terminated I was informed that at a future day it was to be recommenced. While engaged in this labor a valuable mineral spring was opened, and very many papers were transmitted and carefully reported, some of which compose "The Educator," a volume of more than seven hundred pages, carefully prepared for the press by A. E. Newton.*[67]

The work Spear described appears to be that of digging the tunnel (see Chapter 5). The tunnel digging was described in several sources, including the April 12, 1853, *Jamestown Journal*, as taking place by April 1853. Spear, in his autobiography, had already stated that he visited the springs on or about May 10, 1853, and June 10, 1853, and that he subsequently worked on spirit messages regarding the machine. He then went to Cincinnati, and, only then, according to Spear's account, was he called by the spirits to assist in the excavation work on the John Chase farm.

During this time, as previously noted in Oliver F. Chase's paper, Spear also received messages which were eventually gathered into a book edited by A.E. Newton. Entitled, *The Educator*, the book not only taught about the Harmonial philosophy, including the architectural style used, but also further elaborated the seven associations that were to under gird the community: education, health, agriculture, and government being included. The book was both instructive as well as lucrative, as copies were sold to interested readers.

Particularly, note that it appears that Newton was on-site at Kiantone during the course of the excavation work. But this is not conclusive, as Spear recorded that Newton served as editor of *The Educator*. This could mean that that the actual spirit message transcriptions were initially written down by other colleagues and then sent to Newton in Boston for editing. Newton's name was listed in the *Spiritual Telegraph*, a directory for Spiritualist mediums, lecturers, journal editors, and other Spiritualist roles. Placed under the category, *Public Lecturers*, Newton was described as:

Editor of the New England Spiritualist, will respond to the calls of those who may desire his services as a lecturer of the Facts [sic] and Philosophy [sic] of Spiritualism. Address No.15 Franklin-street, Boston, Mass.[68]

The various primary accounts are, indeed, confusing. Frankly, I do not think Spear had anything to do with digging the tunnel. My reasons are simple. First, his dating of his own involvement in the project makes no sense. Second, I just do not think this citified New England preacher had the fortitude for the digging project. But why, writing in 1873,[69] would Spear have wanted his readers to think he was one of the tunnel excavators?

The answer to that question, I believe, is found buried in the accounts of Spear and his encounter with William Brittingham and John Chase. In the essay Oliver F. Chase prepared for the 1904 *Centennial History of Chautauqua County,* he stated:

Owing to pecuniary difficulties, the Chase-Brittingham outfit and the Spear contingent did not agree. The spirits gave an edict of nullification and secession from the heretofore union. One hundred seventy-three acres of land was purchased adjacent, in the Town of Kiantone, and christened "The Domain," improvements made, buildings erected, etc., to be run on the community of interest plan not only in spiritual affairs, but in the more earthly conjugal relations, patterned somewhat after the "Oneida Community," [sic, Chase's punctuation and capitalization] then run by John H. Noyes.[70]

Reading those words, the saga begins to come into clearer focus. John Chase and William Brittingham did the initial hard work of exposing the springs, digging the tunnel, and building the hotel, modest by today's standards, but gigantic compared to other nearby structures in Kiantone. Chase and Brittingham labored[71] hard in order to profit from their investment with the hotel and their healing water and salve sales. Spear, and an array of other mediums, made a couple of visits to the springs to test their spiritual healing possibilities. When Chase and Brittingham realized that Spear wanted in on the profits, a rift occurred. The following passage describes the fallout:

> *Impressed with the perfect fitness of the place for the designs they contemplated, Mr. Spear and his friends entered into an agreement with Messrs. Chase and Brittingham to pursue their explorations, settle upon certain portions of the land, and possess themselves of an appropriate share of the wealth they expected to realize; but when the astounded proprietors of the district heard of the magnificent prospective views mapped out by the enthusiastic clairvoyants, they began to believe that the untold mines of wealth which their new neighbors deigned to realize were just as well reserved in their own hands; hence, they curtly "backed out" of the agreement and left the baffled seers to pursue their researches elsewhere.[72]*

The result of this was that Spear's group purchased land adjacent to that of John Chase and Brittingham. The newcomers announced that springs found on their land also possessed healing properties. Subsequently, they established their own Spiritualist colony, the Domain.

Many of the Kiantone accounts and histories lump together into one story the revealing of the springs and digging the tunnel. But, a careful analysis of primary records provides a different scenario. Chase and Brittingham had their little business straddling the border of New York and Pennsylvania, while Spear and his group encamped some few yards to the east along the creek in Kiantone, NY. Thus, the two establishments existed side by side.

Another event may have also given Chase and Brittingham cause to think that Spear and his group were trying to infringe on their healing water business. Some time after the spring was opened by the two partners, but before the tunnel was dug, Thaddeus Sheldon obtained a sample of the water which he took to New York City for analysis by *Dr. James P. Greaves.* Dr. Greaves subsequently analyzed the water, visited the springs and sent his analysis to *Dr. J. F. Gray*, a physician in Milwaukee, Wisconsin in a letter dated January 24, 1853. Both men were Spiritualists, and Dr. Greaves' report was subsequently published in the 1853 *Spiritual Telegraph*, presumably with Sheldon's permission.

Dr. Greaves wrote of visiting both Chase and Brittingham on site at the Chase farm just over the border from Kiantone. He also referred to Brittingham as a *magnetizer.* This could have meant a reference to either Brittingham's personality or his occupation, the latter as in one who manufactures magnets. My initial hunch was that the latter was correct, given Brittingham's interest in the effects of negative and positive polarities. However, as I read various other sources, I learned that 19th Century Spiritualism used the word, magnetizer, to describe various persons who used healing techniques involving negative and positive polarities. It should also be noted that theories about using negative and positive polarities are still valued by some natural medicine practitioners today.

Greaves also offered a lengthy account of how the spring was dug, and then offered his analysis of the water as being highly alkaline, sufficient to raise bread and biscuits and make them very light.[73] In addition, he mentioned being aware that someone was doing a chemical analysis, but stated that he did not know the results of that study. Greaves offered the information that excavating the spring was accomplished by September 1, 1852, and that the waters had proven successful in healing several diseases and conditions, including "fevers, dyenepeia, pneumonia, rheumatism, inflammations of the throat, burns and scalds, erysipelas, scarlatina, etc."[74]

There were some overlapping interests in the tunnel digging initiative by persons who would, in time, become part of Spear's Harmonia community. Cheney stated in his eyewitness account that the tunnel cost over $6,000 to build. He also indicated that the money was put up by several persons including Dr. Mayhue [*sic*, or *Abel*, which is the name appearing in other primary resources] Underhill, Horace Fenton, John Sterling, and Thaddeus Sheldon.

Later, in 1858, a *New York Daily Tribune* reporter described the tunnel as follows: "Unfortunately for those who would like to make an internal inspection, it is brim-full [*sic*] of water."[75] The article does shed additional light, however, on the original funding for the tunnel.

The excavation was made at the expense of Thaddeus Sheldon, who for several years was known as one of the wealthiest and most enterprising commercial men in Western New York. It is said that the excavation was made in pursuit of treasures buried in the bowels of the earth, he was sunk [sic] about $20,000. So say his old friends.[76]

After writing about his role in the tunnel excavation work, Spear never mentioned Kiantone again in his autobiography, except to say that he wrote the biography at Kiantone, which would have placed him there about 1872 or 1873.[77] Some sources note his presence in Kiantone at various times leading up to and including 1860,[78] but Spear never spent long periods of time at Kiantone. His returning to Kiantone to write his memoirs indicates, I believe, that this place had significant meaning in his life. Otherwise, why would he have returned there to write his autobiography?

How does Spear's account compare with other eyewitness accounts of the creation of the perpetual motion machine and the digging of the springs and tunnel? Eyewitness Wilbert Northrop offered no information about these subjects. But Mark Cheney recalled quite a few details about the tunnel, including an adventurous escapade with his brother.

At this time [1853] they dug a subterranean passage on the Pennsylvania and New York line, 270 feet, at 45 degrees, 7 feet high and 6 feet wide, cast up with oak plank. None but the workmen were admitted, but on one occasion my brother and self on a hunting trip stopped there, found the door unlocked, went into the dark passage, groped our way long, stepped off, missed the track, fell twelve feet, struck in the mud. Not hurt. Saw a dim light 250 feet down, saw something coming toward us, long flowing beard and flaming eyes. We were scared near to death, our teeth chattered with fright. There was no retreat. Right onto us it came. We shrieked out, when we saw it was Mr. Jones, an acquaintance, a workman, who was at work there on the pumps. We then went on down the 227 feet, there being oak steps all the way. It was a wonderful experience. Have never seen anything so wonderful.[79]

Added to this detailed, but rather comical, report was another eyewitness account written by a local newspaper reporter. In regards to the curative powers of the spring water, the reporter seemed unable to resist writing sarcastic doggerel as follows:

The process is by electrical polarity. All diseases are either "positive" or "negative!" Find whether the disease is positive or negative. If positive, apply the negative water; if negative, apply the positive water. And there you have it! Oh, how contemptible now is all your learned wrangling about cauterizing, scarifying, and phlebotomizing; your tepidations, urgations, and anti-adulterations, your phasms, spasms, and cataplasms; your "packs", quacks, and ipecacs! The ills of mortal life are all simplified and classified. They are either positive or negative – hot or cold. The whole world of Physics is in a nutshell, labeled, "Chase and Brittingham," and there you are! Positive or negative?[80]

Evidently, the *Jamestown Journal* editor found the above passage as amusing as I did. Is it reprinted verbatim in another editorial dated, December 2, 1853.

How effective were the waters for healing? That is a difficult question to answer, since it is a question of both science and faith. Chief Cornplanter, as we saw in Chapter 2, believed in the waters' healing properties. Maybe they did have healing qualities, or, perhaps, not. Maybe folks were healed because of the attributes of the well-researched *placebo effect*. This occurs when some people in a controlled experiment receive a sugar pill instead of the actual medicine. Some of the group taking this bogus medicine may be healed simply because they believe they will be healed. On the other hand, Kiantone's healing waters can also be evaluated through this additional tidbit from Oliver F. Chase's eye witness account:

> *These waters were reputed to have medicinal value. The scheme of boiling down the water in huge sap kettles was resorted to, and the sediment or powder put up in small wooden turned boxes and labeled, "A Spiritual Cure All." We call to memory the Chase boys, Dwight, Oscar, and Gilman, who run the outfit, and when the powder did not boil down fast enough, had recourse to the blue clay bank beside the creek.*[81]

Adding clay to the water, of course, would make it boil down to salve more quickly. Boys, after all, will be boys! And, what Dad doesn't know, so much the better!

A MIDNIGHT PROCESSION

Oliver F. Chase gave a description of a peculiar procession that took place, although he offered no mention of the date, other than "once on a time".[82] Chase admitted that he did not personally view the event, but reported, in outline form, how it was described to him:

> *Occasion – the ushering of a new dispensation of freedom of women from masculine tyranny; time- midnight, musical accompaniment, bells, horns, tin pans; costumes – nightgowns.*[83]

Undoubtedly, such a demonstration, possibly a bit of midsummer night's madness, in the narrow confines of the Kiantone Valley, would not have gone unnoticed by the neighbors.

There is a considerably large amount of documentation about the unique architecture that was used at the Domain. Several sources mentioned that Harmonia was largely a summer colony. Winters in this part of New York State are very harsh, with frequent, sometimes waist-deep, snows and harsh winds. Harmonia's cottages would never have been sufficient for winter. Still, despite their lack of "snow-worthiness", the structures were, indeed, unique.

Oliver Chase, who helped build the summer homes along with Mark Cheney, gave a helpful description of their design.

Ten or twelve cottages, square, round and octagon, were built, these were divided into rooms, painted the colors of the rainbow; one room was especially devoted to the shattered remains of "The Electric Motor...[84]

Given the detailed accounts of the cottages that appear in many secondary sources, it is surprising that Chase offered such a cursory description of them. Mark Cheney's description offered yet fewer clues. What did catch Chase's boyhood imagination, however, was the pageantry of the summer colony, which he described as ". . . tents, round and octagon houses of green, blue and red rooms of caves and springs, and camp sites. . . now as obliterated to the observer as the glories of storied cities of the past. . . nothing but ruins remain."[85] Oliver F. Chase wrote this essay as a grown man in 1904, with whitened mustache, as his photo accompanying the article indicates. Yet, it was delightful how he reverted back to his childhood sense of wonder as he related this eyewitness tale.

Seeing such a colorful spectacle in the deep green woods, what must the other residents of the Kiantone area have thought of the unusual activities taking place in the little valley?

Once again, the *New York Daily Tribune* article, though written several years after the construction of the cottages, gave more information about their construction. It is a reasonable hunch that the reporter, who attended a Spiritualist convention at Kiantone, asked questions about the structures found there. Here, though, we are faced with the question of whether the newspaper reporter cited what he saw with sarcasm, or if he simply had a tendency towards grandiosity. Consider the words he used to describe the Domain:

> " ... *here stood its capital city. That city was magnificent beyond all earthly comparison. The prevailing style of the architecture was copied from Nature. Every building, public or private, had a circular ground-plan, and internally it was vaulted or painted blue in imitation of the ethereal canopy. Windows were not in use. Every building was lighted during the day by a gorgeous and dazzling brilliant solar light, and in the night by a pale lunar lamp, together with almost innumerable stellar lights bespangling the whole cerulean vaulted roof and walls of the edifice. Externally, the city was incomparably green and magnificent. It was profusely adorned with lofty domes, turrets, spires, colonnades and battlements, all of which were wrought in a style of ornate beauty and splendor never before nor since known to architectural skill. The city was also beautified with walks, pleasure grounds, and gardens, wherein the hand of cultivation had brought forth the greenest and softest of rewards, the most symmetrical shrubs and trees, and the rarest and richest flowers that ever gladdened the vision of mortal man.*[86]

Upon reading this description, the only viable response is, "Nu uh!" the wonderful Americanism better translated as "Oh, for pity's sake, no!" Glass windows may not have been used, but some kind of oilcloth or shutter system must have been incorporated into the buildings to keep out the fierce spring and summer rains. As for "dazzling brilliant solar light", well, there are some days like that in Western New York, but the region is also known for its foggy mornings and dark grey days. I have a hard time believing that there was much in the way of "lofty domes, turrets, spires, colonnades, and battlements", unless, perhaps, some children were present and making sand castles. There was perhaps as much fantasy as fact to the reporter's version.

Fantasy is, however, a powerful stimulator of the human mind and spirit. Mel Feather, a retired Frewsburg Central School history teacher, mentioned my research to a friend, Norma Gagliano. She promptly offered him a copy of an article about Harmonia printed in the Northeast, PA, *Sea Breeze,* that included an illustration of what part of the proposed Harmonia city might look like (Illustration 1). Astonishingly, Mrs. Gagliano had found the article just recently at a yard sale! I had never before seen the article, so I spent some considerable time trying to track down the author and illustration artist, *Jim Towery.* but I could not locate him. In time, it occurred to me that his drawing featured Harmonia's proposed tower-like structures and I wondered if he had taken a special interest in the project because of his last name. In the end, I determined that the article was probably from the mid-20th Century. I place it here in hopes that the creator, if still alive, will appreciate once again seeing his art in print.

An elaborate description of the octagon cottages is found in Gregory Yaw's academic paper written in 1972. Yaw carefully studied *The Educator,* the vast compendium of information Spear received from the spirit world that directed the establishment of

Illustration 1

the Domain. From this work, Yaw developed this description of the cottages:

> *The general requisites of the new architecture were that it must have a consecrated apartment for seclusion and meditation and that it must be circular or oval in form because the rounded human body is not in equilibrium with angular environment. The universal law that "THE BODY IS A HOUSE [sic]; and as man approximate to its laws, in the same ratio he becomes a <u>natural</u> [sic] constructor," is extended to the details of architectural organization. The form of the model house approximates that of the human body. The interior is arranged with a culinary department in the basement corresponding to the intestines, a dome on the top representing the mind, a dining room corresponding to the stomach, a worship room modeled on the ordinary sitting rooms representing the lungs, and a hollow tube in the center for communication from the basement to the dome (with sliding apparatus, spiral staircases, bell-wires, speaking tubes, water pipes, etc.) corresponding to the spinal column and its nerves, blood vessels, etc.*[87]

It should be noted that some magazine articles (secondary resources) include a photo of the last remaining octagon cottage, taken in the late 1890s. I was also both told and read that the cottages rested on foundations made of heavy glass bottles. This foundation allowed for rotating the entire cottage for solar heating and light, as well as for cooling it on hot days. Remaining bottles could be found in the valley during the first part of the 1900s, but none can be found today.

Finally, Illustration 2 is a drawing of one cottage that appeared in several of the resources. It was drawn by Viola G. Cushman in 1907, presumably when the cottages were still standing.

Illustration 2

A Journalist - Why would the *New York Daily Tribune* writer go to such lengths to describe a few un-winterized shacks in a backwoods valley along a small creek? The *Tribune* was owned and edited by *Horace Greeley,* who also wrote for the paper. Surprisingly, Greeley, the renowned journalist, had family ties to the area, as well as an interest in both Spiritualist and utopian matters. No doubt, he was fascinated to learn about Spear's community, especially since it had taken root in Chautauqua County.

Greeley was born in *Amherst, NH* in 1811, and, formal schooling ended, he apprenticed with a newspaper in *Pultney, VT* at age fourteen. While apprenticed, his family, never prosperous, moved to *Erie County, PA,* about twenty-five miles west of Kiantone and just over the state line from *Clymer, NY.* He finally caught up with his frontier family after walking about 400 miles across New York State. He worked in the newspaper business for a short time in

Jamestown, *Lodi* (now *Gowanda*), and *Erie, PA*, before making his way to New York City.

Greeley was an adamant abolitionist and supported many of the proposed social reforms of his day, including advocating against capital punishment. A literate and intellectual man, he was also involved in politics, first with the *Whig Party* and then with the Republican Party.

With an eye to the emerging philosophies and belief systems of his day, many of Greeley's newspaper staff were part of the *Transcendentalist Movement*, as expressed in the works of writers such as *Ralph Waldo Emerson* and *Henry David Thoreau*. The movement was a popular early 19th Century literary and philosophical initiative that used intuition to achieve an ideal spirituality that moved beyond empirical and scientific data. An idealist and egalitarian, Greeley, ". . . popularized the communitarian ideas of Fourier who, along with Robert Owen, was a great utopian socialist, and invested in a Fourier utopian community at Red Bank, New Jersey".[88]

Greeley knew the Fox Sisters well and believed they did not cause the rappings. Perhaps the only thing surprising about the *New York Daily Tribune* taking an interest in Harmonia is that Greeley sent a staff reporter to do the story, rather than covering it himself. Nevertheless, he took a significant interest in Harmonia and dedicated considerable column space to Harmonia's 1858 convention.

OCCUPATIONS

When they were not busy digging in the ground or executing their architectural plans, just what did the members of the Harmonia community do? We can surmise that, because they believed that the spring waters had healing properties, they must

have conducted various kinds of healing rituals, most likely connected with séances. It is likely that some persons journeyed
great distances to come to the healing waters. This must have
necessitated providing some arrangements for accommodations,
including meals, while they were at Kiantone. Given the nature of
the Domain, there were also probably long hours given to lectures,
teaching sessions, and conversations.

At the Domain, Spear and others received numerous spirit
messages, an occupation that must have consumed considerable
amounts of time. Those who served as scribes, or *amanuenses*, likewise spent time writing down and transcribing the messages as
the mediums spoke them. No doubt there was considerable review
of the work, if not actual editing, following these trance events.

The Domain community endeavored to feed themselves and
create products for sale. As Oliver F. Chase notes, "Strawberries,
raspberries and blackberries were raised, and a grove of 'Osier
Willows' planted for basket weaving...".[89] However, agriculture was
never a very prosperous activity for the group.

Finally, it is important to remember that Harmonia was about
more than Spiritualism. Spear and his followers brought with
them a deep commitment to the Abolition Movement. Kiantone,
located on the Pennsylvania border, was on a route of the Underground Railroad. It, therefore, seems likely that the members
of the Domain participated, to some degree, as conductors, or
at least helpers, for those making the journey to freedom. If it
seems odd that there are no primary documents describing this
activity, remember that the Fugitive Slave Law made assisting
runaway slaves a federal offence. My strong hunch is that there
was considerable activity of this sort, but, of course, that hunch
cannot be proved.

Free Love - Despite winter snows, internal discord, and competing egos, one thing, and one thing alone, doomed the Harmonia
experiment. Thaddeus Sheldon was deeply convinced, as noted
above, that, *There is a Law of Love,* and that this love should rule all
human endeavors. He probably never anticipated that his contro-
versial views about love would eventually destroy Harmonia.

As we have seen, Harmonia was not unique in engaging in the
experiment of Free Love. Noyes' Oneida Community and other
utopian groups in the mid-19th Century also embraced various
expressions of this philosophy. This, in turn, caused each of these
groups to receive varying amounts of criticism. At Kiantone, criticism of what appeared to many as an erotic alternative lifestyle,
embraced by some of its members, but not all of them, was ever
lurking in the shadows, ready to become a crisis.

Sheldon believed that a man could find spiritual wholeness in
a woman. If a man married a woman who could not give him this,
then he was free to divorce her and continue his search. Sheldon
viewed such divorce as an unfortunate, messy, but necessary occurrence. Consequently, he also believed that prior to marriage,
men and women should simply experiment with each other, in a
sexual manner, to see if they were compatible spiritual partners.
This was the style of Free Love that was embraced, at least by some
of the Domain's members. One wonders what Sheldon's wives,
particularly his second wife, thought of such a philosophy. Again,
there appears to be no historical record concerning the thoughts
of either of his wives.

At Kiantone, the origins of this radical social system were
found not only in Sheldon's philosophies, but also in the culture of
the Celtic Indians who supposedly had lived there long ago. The
discovery of this culture, of course, had been through a fortune-
teller. Thus, anyone who dismissed the validity of such insight

might have dismissed the Celtic Indian version of Free Love as well. But again, during the 19th Century, a variety of groups, including the Mormons, Oneida Community, and the Kingdom of Mattias, were challenging the basic understanding of monogamous love as best expressed in the covenant of traditional marriage. Harmonia's interest, therefore, does not stand alone, nor can it be attributed solely to the practice of either Spiritualism or an ethereal, long-ago Celtic Indian culture at Kiantone. What is important is that the negative reaction to Harmonia's Free Love contributed to its demise and cast a pall over Spiritualism.

Many Spiritualists were furious with Harmonia for the wanton way many of its members engaged in Free Love. This was an issue that would not go away. Writing eleven years latter, Emma Hardinge expressed her venom towards the actions taken at the Domain:

To no point to we trace the most baseless allegation [sic, that all Spiritualists practiced Free Love] more clearly than to the Kiantone community. It would be unfit to assert that all the Spiritualists who there assembled, professed, or even favored these opinions, but it would be equally false to truth and the cause of Spiritualism to deny, that from this place, and at the time of the settlement narrated above, the propagandism of these opinions became most mischievously associated with Spiritualism, bringing a scandal and reproach on the heads of thousands of innocent persons, who loathed and repudiated the doctrine, and causing thousands of others to shrink back from the investigation of a belief that was so strangely associated with the most repulsive features of communism.[90]

It should be noted that the "communism" of which Hardinge writes is not, of course, the social system as experienced in the

20th Century, but rather is a reference to the utopian, communitarian expressions of community life as seen in the 19th Century Shakers and Oneida Community. What cannot be denied, however, is that Hardinge and other Spiritualist leaders clearly blamed Spiritualism's faltering progress in the 1860's and thereafter on Harmonia and John Murray Spear. Most likely, that faltering was largely related to the end of the Civil War and its great number of disturbing deaths, which had driven many folks to Spiritualism for comfort. Nevertheless, Free Love was obviously singled out to take the blame for impeding the growth of Spiritualism.

Conventions

When discussing the *convention* at Kiantone, it is important to note that there were actually two separate events, each designated as a convention. The first, which probably took place in 1853, was small in nature. It was most likely the occasion when John Murray Spear came to discern the worth and usefulness of the spring waters first exposed by John Chase and William Brittingham.

Mark Cheney remembered both conventions. Of the first he related, "In 1853, they erected a large open auditorium seating 800 or more, for lectures and public speaking".[91] Despite the large auditorium, the numbers attending were probably quite small. The "they" that Cheney refers to are most likely Spear, John Chase, William Brittingham, and the other Spiritualists that accompanied Spear from Cleveland, including Horace Fenton, Dr. Abel Underhill, *Samuel Trent, Dr. and Mrs. Britt, William E. Dunn, Emily Hikox, Caroline Sykes, Carol Fuller,* and *Hannah F. M. Brown,* all of whom Spear lists as going with him from Cleveland to Kiantone.[92]

The second, more formal, *Kiantone Spiritualist Convention,* took place from September 15 to September 17, 1858, on a weekend. We really do not know whether this event was planned by a national group or not. The philosophy of Free Love, for better or worse, defined the message of this gathering. Whatever way Free Love was presented at Harmonia in the community's early days, at this convention it reached its zenith.

As noted above, because of the area's typically very short summers, people came and went at Harmonia depending on the seasons. John Murray Spear was no exception. Thus, in 1854, we find him in Boston, attending the June 2, 1854, *Massachusetts Spiritual Convention.*[93] On March 7-8, 1855, there was a *Central National Organization of Spiritualists* event in Boston. It is quite likely that Spear attended that meeting, as his signature is included on the notice that went out to publicize that gathering.[94]

However, in the spring of 1858, Spear returned to Kiantone intensely involved in his own Free Love experiment. He moved to Kiantone for the summer, perhaps even intending to take up permanent residency at the Domain. Having left his wife and children, he came to Kiantone, built a new octagon cottage, and lived there with *Mrs. Caroline Hinckley*, a divorced woman. This behavior, at least according to Thaddeus Sheldon, would have been perfectly acceptable within the Harmonia community. However, it is impossible, by today's rather relaxed sexual standards in the United States, to understand the scandal caused by this liaison. It was met with scorn by neighbors in the hamlet of Kiantone, regional on-lookers, and even other Spiritualists who did not embrace such radical behavior. There is no doubt that Spear and Hinckley's relationship was viewed widely as a disgrace. Spear's behavior in this matter would taint him and undermine the remainder of his Spiritualist ministry. This, then, was the Domain's societal environment for the convention about to unfold.

During the convention, a large number of people descended on the little hamlet of Kiantone and the Harmonia grounds along

Kiantone Creek. The weather that weekend was typically change-able, as it often is in Western New York, with a chilly Friday, a pleasant Saturday, and a splendid Sunday awash with autumn's bright blue sky.

Although Chase and Brittingham, long ago, had disassociated their operation from that of Spear's, it is likely that Brittingham, given the opportunity to make a considerable profit, made his hotel available for paying guests. Still, it is difficult to imagine how room and board, let alone transportation, was provided for such an event. Different histories record the number in attendance anywhere from 4,000 to 10,000. Did they come on foot, by wagon, by train,[95] or did they travel up the Conewango Creek or take a packet boat on the Erie or Genesee canals?[96] The best answer is that, if they came from any great distance, they probably used a combination of two or more of these forms of transportation. The last leg to Kiantone, however, had to be either by horseback, stagecoach, buggy, or on foot.

I had great consternation about where folks attending the convention stayed and how they were fed, not to mention other creature comforts. The valley just seems too small to have accom-modated such a large group. Then I talked with Gregory Yaw, the Jamestown attorney who wrote his college honors paper about Kiantone. His answer to how so many people could come together in little Kiantone was a simple one. He said, "Well, I always thought it must have been a lot like Woodstock!" After some deliberation, I had to admit that Yaw was probably correct in his assumption. Of course, some of the conventioneers were from nearby farms and towns, so they probably brought picnics to eat and then returned home at night.

Both the *Jamestown Weekly Journal* and the *New York Daily Tribune* sent reporters to the convention. It is interesting that persons from Spear's General Assembly are not listed as attending, with the exception of *Mary Gardner, Thaddeus Sheldon,* and *John Sterling,* the first two living nearby and Sterling coming from Cleveland.

John Murray Spear, of course, attended. Others included *Mr. Coddling, Mr. Loveland, Dr. Wellington, Dr. Newton, Mrs. Britt, Mrs. Branch, Mrs. Lewis, Mrs. Trantrom,* and *Miss Thompson.* Of these, a *J. S. Loveland* appears as having attended the Massachusetts Spiritual Convention in 1854,[97] but there is no proof that he is the same "Mr. Loveland" who attended Kiantone's convention. *Caroline Lewis,* from Cleveland, also attended. She is referred to variously in the two newspaper articles as "Carrie" and "Popcorn", the latter a rather charming nickname that might have either described her character or her favorite snack food. Dr. Newton is probably A.E. Netown, the editor of *The Educator.* Mrs. Britt was a speaker, as was Mr. Coddington. Mrs. Tantram spoke, but only against the violent protests of Mrs. Lewis, who was also described as the "President of the Convention" by the *New York Daily Tribune* reporter.

The same reporter included a rather hilarious description of Mrs. Lewis' reaction to Mrs. Tantram's speech, saying that when Mrs. Lewis tried to prevent Mrs. Tantram from speaking, Mrs. Tantram "... gave her right arm a violent sweep, which sent Mrs. Lewis reeling across the stage".[98] If women's rights at that time meant that women had the right to a slugfest, then they certainly achieved their aim.

The name, "Mrs. Tantram", caught my eye. For a long time, I wondered if "Tantram" was really the woman's last name, or one that the reporter made up to suit her behavior, a vaguely disguised spelling of "tantrum". Once again, Karen Livsey's excellent genealogical research turned up some fascinating possibilities. The surname, "Trantum", showed up in an 1850 Census record as a family living in *West Seneca, Erie County, NY.* The name was listed with a property title, "Middle Ebenezer", a communal community established in 1843, by German immigrants. The Middle Ebenezer community left Western New York in 1845, and set up a communitarian settlement in *Amana, IA.* That group bears the distinction of being the only such community in the United States that is still growing and today, has about 1,800 members. However, six people were listed in the 1850 Census record of the Trantum family. Included is *Elizabeth*, age 55, who may fit the description recorded by *New York Daily Tribune* reporter as "a pale, haggard-looking woman", since she would have been 63 years old at the time, which was an elderly age in that era. The reporter also noted that she was from Pennsylvania, where a family named Trantums shows up in the 1860 Census in Warren County, PA. The overall research is inconclusive regarding the woman's actual identify, but my gut tells me the woman may have been, at one time, associated with the Middle Ebenezer Community.

On the first day of the convention, Friday, few people were in attendance. Only two or three spoke, but their names were not recorded. This probably meant that they did not have much to say, other than the typical welcoming speeches and words of instruction that typify the beginnings of such events.

A large number of people attended on Saturday. Several speakers were available and each wanted to be first to address the convention. The principal speech came from Mr. Coddington, described as a "trance medium" by the *New York Daily Tribune* reporter. His speech supported Free Love. The reporter's writing about this speech follows:

He insisted that the "Harmonial Philosophy" was elevating man from ignorance and superstition and fitting him for the duties of "Spirit Life." What the world needs, said Mr. Coddington (or, rather, said the spirit through Mr. C. [sic, reporter's abbreviation], is freedom – freedom of thought, freedom of speech, freedom of action, and freedom of the affections, was the most important. The marriage institution was slavery, and should be abolished. Those groaning beneath the galling fetters of matrimony, should be freed at once and left to bestow their affection when and where they pleased. Our hearts were our own property, and it was not the province of society to direct, restrict, or hinder their impulses or aspirations. In a word, the spirit speaking through Mr. Coddington, was decidedly in favor of Free Love.[99]

There was no mention of Mr. Coddington's first name. This is particularly interesting. The name, "Coddington", does not appear in all the various lists of mediums, healers, Spiritualist publications editors, or lecturers and other related categories that were published from 1854 to the early 1860's. Perhaps he was a local person, so well known to folks in Kiantone that only his last name was needed for identification.

Next spoke a young woman from Cattaraugus, NY. She spoke in a trance, accompanied by seemingly hysterical writhings and contortions. Her address, like Mr. Coddington's, was about Free Love. She spoke, or rather, shouted, saying:

Free Love! free love! [sic, reporter used small capitalization] It is God's law, it is heaven's command; let not man presume to chain and imprison the heart, lead captive the young affections, and quench the divine scintillations of holy love.[100]

The only appropriate response to the young woman's speech is, "Whew!" The *New York Daily Tribune* reporter wrote that several other persons spoke to the convention on Saturday, but he did not understand what they said, as he found it thoroughly clouded in Spiritualist language and jargon.

Another reporter, from the *Jamestown Weekly Journal*, filed a somewhat different account on September 24, 1858.

> *When I reached the Convention on the P.M. of Saturday, I found a motley crowd, with curious eyes, watching the vehement declaration of the President, Mrs. Carrie ("Popcorn") Lewis of Cleveland, who was rehearsing the divine messages of the "spirits" given through John M. Spear, the accredited (by some) link between the material and the spiritual world. Such ranting mysticism and extravagance, such verbiage and nonsense, it has not been my lot to hear of, since the Babel period.*[101]

The reporter continued, saying that the essence of the message was Free Love, which he took to be a considerable threat to the orthodox understanding of the family structure. He also noted that a *Mrs. Haley* from Chicago spoke about the new social order, which would be based on harmony. The reporter's comments about the next speaker were direct and also rather humorous:

> *Mr. S. C. Hewitt said he would explain what they had proposed do. He had not a clear idea himself, as the harangue showed, and so he could not explain.*[102]

The reporter noted that the rest of the day's speeches were also about Free Love.

Sunday was largely taken over by, "long-bearded gentry",[103] who lectured about Spiritualism. Their messages were decidedly sedate compared to those speakers who believed they were possessed of spirits that wished to speak through them to the crowd. This was finally interrupted by the afore-mentioned Mrs. Tantram, who in addition to her wrestling match with Mrs. Lewis, spoke passionately about Free Love. The reporter ended his narrative of her speech with these words:

She finally ran into the most abominable Free-Lovism, using disgusting, obscene language and descending to vulgar and filthy expressions. Her husband and brothers, who were on the ground, carried her away, then order was once more restored.[104]

Obviously, speeches at the convention were both informative and entertaining!

Dr. Wellington of Jamestown spoke in the afternoon. He was clearly against Free Love and simply affirmed his belief in Spiritualism. It is interesting to note that there was a Dr. Wellington listed in the 1860 *Fourth Annual Spiritual Register,* as having an, "Institute", named after him. In the 1861 register, however, the school was denoted as "suspended in preparations for new arrangements".[105] This same Dr. O. H. Wellington was also listed in the 1861 *Spiritual Register* as a "public speaker" in Massachusetts. It could be conjectured that Dr. Wellington, for a time, had an interest in the Kiantone community, as well as nearby Jamestown, but that his educational endeavors in that region did not continue.

Next, John Sterling attempted to speak, but was drowned out by a Mrs. A. M. Britt of St. Louis. Mrs. Britt was as entertaining as any of the other woman speakers who participated in the convention. She had traveled a long distance to Kiantone and she was not about to leave unheard. She was initially on the approved speakers list, but stated that she withdrew her name because she disapproved of how the convention was progressing. When Mrs. Britt decided to speak, she drew the listeners away from the speakers' platform to another area in the valley. There she declared her disapproval of everything that had taken place at the convention. Her speech turned out to be the high point of the entire three days!

Mrs. Britt stated that her deceased mother had become her guardian angel and was present as Mrs. Britt spoke to the thousands gathered in the Kiantone Valley. She then declared that there was actually a large group of spirit witnesses present with her in the valley at that very moment. Mrs. Britt continued her impromptu speech, stating that humans are depraved until they turn to the good. Her speech was actually quite reminiscent of the teachings of the Christian Apostle Paul. Paul wrote in Hebrews 12:1 of our being "surrounded by a cloud of witnesses". The apostle also taught that humans are confronted with an inherent dual nature, good and bad, and the promise of heaven for those who chose the good.

Whatever the source of her ideas, Mrs. Britt's words struck some chord of truth in her listeners. Initially, many rough characters tried to drown out Mrs. Britt with rude shouting, but she spoke kindly to them and soon they were hanging onto every word she spoke. The *New York Daily Tribune* reporter noted that Mrs. Britt was "an orator of rare power and accomplishment",[106] and concluded the telling of her address with these words:

Mrs. Britt's speech, saying nothing of the sentiment expressed
– and even that was not very censurable – was far more eloquent
and impressive than any other feminine address to which I

ever listened. The thousands that heard it were lavish in their expressions of gratification. Several ladies came with streaming eyes to thank the orator and yield assent to the sentiments and opinions advanced.[107]

Mrs. Britt's speech, as chronicled by the *New York Daily Tribune* reporter, appeared to be a blending of Spiritualist and traditional Christian teachings, augmented by common sense and dignity. Suffice it to say that the speech resonated well with her listeners, especially given some of the convention's other antics. Her words also reminded me of words one of my bishops used to recite frequently:

> *Heretic, rebel, a thing to pout,*
>
> *He drew a circle and left me out.*
>
> *But love and I had the wit to win,*
>
> *We drew a circle and took him in.*

The *New York Daily Tribune* article concluded with these words:

Following Mrs. B.'s [sic] speech, a statement was made of the plan of a harmonial city. According to that statement, a costly temple is to be reared; colleges, seminaries, and churches are to be erected; dwellings and other buildings are to be constructed, and then is to be done whatever is necessary to complete the populous, wealthy, prosperous, magnificent, and harmonial city. This enterprise is already begun.[108]

The *Jamestown Weekly Journal* identified one of the "long-beard-ed gentry" who spoke on Sunday as Thaddeus Sheldon, who spoke "with undoubted sincerity about Spiritualism".[109] Next followed a very entertaining description of Carrie Lewis' speech for the day:

> *The flippant, blushing Cleopatra walks onto the stand in the midst of a popular crowd gloating over the conceptions of an impure fantasy, and – a woman – discourses on a subject sacred to the library of the physician or the holy of holies of the family.*[110]

The *Jamestown Weekly Journal* reporter then noted another "long-bearded gentry" member, Mr. Newton, who ". . . made a con-servative plea on Spiritualism, and its aim to elevate the race".[111] This is an interesting quotation, since the *New York Daily Tribune* reporter cited the aforementioned Mr. Coddington as having said almost the exact same words. Could one of the reporters have been confused as to who was speaking?

With no mention of the afore-mentioned "Mrs. Tantram", the *Jamestown Weekly Journal* reporter then described Mrs. Britt and her eloquent dismissal of the Free Love philosophy. Throughout the convention, with the exception of Mrs. Britt's speech, there was an ever-present tension between what the men were saying and what the women were saying. The *Jamestown Weekly Journal* reporter summarized that conflict, which colored the overall impact of the convention, with these words:

> *The other proceedings I cannot follow. These men seemed utterly crazy with their absurd vagaries; and it was heart-sickening to see women – the angel-keepers of the spotless properties of life and social intercourse, plunging into the abyss of Free Loveism [sic], and*

showing its offensive details to the crowd. Shouting, intemperance,
and bad manners came with the multitude.[112]

And so the 1858 Kiantone Spiritualist Convention drew to a close. It is intriguing to imagine Thaddeus Sheldon, sitting in his elegant carriage on the side of the road, watching those who had attended the convention as they streamed out of the valley towards home, ruminating on his own words, *There is a Law of Love.* Had Free Love been made manifest at the convention? Had Free Love been loosed though the public speeches and private conversations around the campfires? What was the next step in this journey of Free Love and the Harmonia community?

Even Thaddeus Sheldon, ever the visionary, could not imagine where Harmonia was headed next.

CHAPTER 9

THE RIVER VOYAGE

THEY SAILED TO NEW ORLEANS AND BACK AGAIN?

Occasionally while writing this chapter, I found myself humming the Beatles' song, "We all live in a yellow submarine, a yellow submarine, a yellow submarine". But then, I would abruptly return to the reality of 1859, a year whose events set the course for a terrible chapter in American history. The Harmonia community found itself smack dab in the middle of those events.

It was not supposed to be that way. John Murray Spear and his colleagues had planned the 1858 Kiantone Spiritualist Convention in hopes that it would be an uplifting spiritual and educational event. It was designed to display the finest aspects of Spiritualism and extend the grandiose vision of Harmonia to a much wider group of people. Instead, the event had been, at best, somewhat boring, and, at worst, flamboyantly radical and divisive. There was discord at Harmonia after the convention. This was painfully obvious, years later, when John Murray Spear made no mention of the convention in his autobiography. The omission strongly signaled his dissatisfaction, perhaps even his embarrassment, with the whole thing.

A careful reading of the *Sheldon Papers* and other related documents from the remainder of 1858 and into 1859 offers an outline of what happened next. The *New York Daily Tribune* article about the convention had been a devastating report. John Sterling, one of Harmonia's strongest supporters, reacted to it, not by writing a letter to the *Tribune*, but rather, to the *Spiritual Telegraph*, the Spiritualist newspaper. The editor of that publication printed Sterling's letter and responded to it in the same issue.[113]

Sterling's basic contention was that Kiantone was merely a summer community with only a handful of people who, busy with clearing land and building structures, did not really have time for Free Love. The *Spiritual Telegraph* editor was not put off by Sterling's explanation. He scoffed at the idea that Mrs. Hinckley's pregnancy, which most folks attributed to her relationship with Spear, was some kind of immaculate conception. He also made sarcastic reference to the source of the pregnancy by writing that it was, "no more nor less than Spear-ism gone to seed".[114]

Other commentators picked up on the shameless failure of the convention at Kiantone. One of the most devastating editorials follows:

> *This Chautauque [sic] affair is but another manifestation of the spirit which prompts a certain class of fanatics to release themselves from all the restraints which virtuous society imposes; in their specious generalities is concealed a design to adopt practices at which the taste and conscience of the community revolt. They have selected for their association one of the most secluded localities in the state where it is manifestly their purpose to repeat the experiment of Berlin Heights [near Berlin, OH; the scene of a Spiritualist Free Love Colony]. The courage of which they boast is simply the effrontery of impudent men and shameless women; and their vaunted self-development consists in the unlimited gratification of passion and appetite.*[115]

Things had gotten out of control with the convention. A clamp-down of sorts was needed and that is exactly what happened. Gregory Yaw, based on his careful study of the *Sheldon Papers*, described these new constrictions as follows:

After 1858, the Kiantone Harmonia seems to have become a more stable and permanent enterprise. It began to be occupied in the winter as well as the summer. With housing for only thirty persons, it was small compared to other communitarian experiments. . . A more detailed specification of the general rules governing the colony was made. Profane, boisterous, obscene, and indecent language was prohibited. Strict bureaucratic division of labor was maintained. Length of labor (8 hours/day) and times for eating were established for the entire community. A dual monarchy of Thaddeus Sheldon and Carrie Lewis was established to provide decisive and coherent direction to the community. In place of treasure hunts "earnest labor" and "just sacrifice" was required of all members.[116]

Meanwhile, Spear reverted to being a non-permanent resident at Kiantone, coming and going at various times. A restless man, called to what he believed was a missionary ministry, Spear began to sense that the spirits had a new far-flung adventure for him. But, real life interfered with this new vision for a time.

Three months after the convention, Spear was arrested on unspecified charges, though they probably had something to do with his having a legal wife and four children in Boston and a pregnant Spiritualist mistress now at his side. In time, Taddeus Sheldon would have to come to Spear's rescue and provide funds for his legal wife and one child still living at home.

A second legal problem was a lawsuit brought against Spear by Miss Eliza J. Kenney, the Apostle of Government. This was dealt with very cryptically in a letter written to Thaddeus Sheldon on December 28, 1858 by *Dan Gano*, a Spiritualist in *Vine Hill*, near Cincinnati.[117] It is possible that Kenney had begun to see how Free Love was potentially abusive to women. Thaddeus Sheldon taught that a man could engage in a sexual relationship with a woman, without benefit of marriage, to see if in that physical union there was also a spiritual affinity. This *testing* was exactly what Spear had done, leaving his legal wife to fend for herself, while testing both the physical and spiritual attributes of Mrs. Hinckley. Kenney might have retaliated with a civil suit against Spear, fearing that her association with him could have tainted her own reputation. Spear, too, could have sought to take advantage of Miss Kenney by also testing her. In the end, the actual issue remained a mystery, in the sense that it was not committed to letters and reports, but it no doubt contributed to the negativism now defining the Kiantone community.

Leaving the past behind, Spear, in 1859, quite literally launched upon a new venture. Through various mediumistic events, he and his fellow Spiritualists became convinced that their spirit friends were now directing them to undertake a river voyage into the heartland of the United States. The idea presented itself at the end of the 1859 summer session at Harmonia. Several members of the community, including Spear and Mrs. Hinckley, stayed on at the colony through the autumn to plan the adventure.

Once again, these dedicated Spiritualists were willing to undertake a daunting task based on what they believed were the explicit instructions of dead people. The list of departed spirits directing them in this task included some who had lead previous Spear initiatives, such as *Benjamin Franklin, Roger Sherman, John Howard,* and *John Murray.* In addition to these, other spirit-persons

inspiring the impending river voyage included *John Quincy Adams,
Robert Ratoul, Thomas Astor, Emanuel Swedenborg, Robert Fulton, M. De
La Mothe Guyon, Eliz. Frye, Samuel Thompson, John Hancock, Samuel Adams, Patrick Henry, Ellis Gray Loving, William Wilberforce, Granville Sharp,
George Washington,* and *Alexander Hamilton.*

It is always interesting to take a moment to review the occupations and activities these spirits engaged in prior to their physical
deaths. This list is equally fascinating. It is dominated by persons
who were involved in a variety of activities such as the Continental
Congress, the Declaration of Independence, the American Revolutionary War, the presidency, congressional representation, and the
governorship of Massachusetts. Included in this list were *Samuel
Adams, George Washington, John Quincy Adams, Alexander Hamilton,
Patrick Henry,* and *John Hancock.* Some of these patriots supported
the institution of slavery and some did not.

One particularly interesting person was *Alexander Hamilton.*
He served as an *aid-de-camp* to George Washington during the
American Revolutionary War and was later killed in a duel with
Aaron Burr. Adding to his unique status is his identification, among
some historians, as a man who had a predilection for male companionship. This, of course, is hardly news, as such relationships
have frequently occurred throughout history among men serving
for long periods in the military. Still, one wonders if Spear and his
group were aware of Hamilton's purported liaisons, even, perhaps,
considering him to be somewhat of an early partner in the Free
Love movement.

Two of the names on the list did not indicate any reference
when I searched them on the Internet: *Thomas Astor* and *Eliz. Frye.*
The name, *Emanuel Swedenborg,* we have previously met in Chapter
5. *Samuel Thompson* proved to be a challenge, since research indicated two physicians with that name, born just four years apart

and dying the same year. One Samuel Thompson was from South Carolina, fought in the Revolutionary War and owned slaves. He was also among the first White Anglo settlers of Texas, arriving there in 1826. A second physician named Samuel Johnson, more likely to be among the spirits guiding Spear and his colleagues, was born in Massachusetts in 1765. He developed the unconventional (today we would say, *alternative*) *Thompsonian System of Medicine* that incorporated into this therapeutic system herbology, avoidance of cold temperatures, and excessive vomiting as a means of releasing toxins from the body. Such a system was widely used across the American frontier, where physicians were rare. This proves some degree of its efficacy. Since Spear was also interested in alternative healing methods, Thompson's system would have appealed to him.

Three of the apostles were renowned abolitionists. The first two listed below were probably known personally by John Murray Spear. They also both died in 1858, just before the river voyage emerged as part of the spirits' plan for Spear and his fellow Spiritualists. The first of these was *Robert Ratoul* (1778-1858), a *Massachusetts pharmacist* who championed social reforms such as peace, temperance, and eliminating the death penalty as well as serving as an advocate and catalyst for liberal religious beliefs. He was elected to the *United States Congress* because he opposed both extending slavery into the territories and the Fugitive Slave Law.

The second abolitionist was a contemporary of Robert Ratoul, *Ellis Gray Loring* (1803-1858). Mr. Loring tried a case before the *Massachusetts Supreme Court* that resulted in the decision that slaves brought by their masters to Massachusetts, for whatever reason, were declared legally free. He also helped form the first American anti-slavery society in 1833.

Granville Sharp (1735-1813), the third abolitionist, was a *British citizen* thought to be somewhat eccentric, since his abolition activity focused on detailed evaluation of legal procedures involving slavery, as opposed to practical assistance to slaves. His colleagues included John Wesley, Thomas Clarkson, and William Wilberforce.

Next among the apostles was *Robert Fulton* (1765-1815). Fulton is often cited as the inventor of the steamship, but actually he was the first person to put in practice what had been designed previously by others. He also designed the first submarine. Particularly interesting to Spear's voyage is that, together with *Robert Livingston*, Fulton built the first large steamship that successfully traveled from Pittsburgh to New Orleans.

Last among this group of spiritual guides was *M. de la Mothe-Gunyon*. The most likely person who fit this surname preceded by the feminine title was Jeanne-Marie Bouvier de la Mothe-Gunyon, a celebrated 17th *Century French mystic*. Through various stages, she came to the understanding of being fully possessed by God and pure heavenly love. Seen as a threat to the traditional *Roman Catholic Church* and the reign of *Louis XIV*, M. de la Mothe-Gunyon was imprisoned in the Bastille for seven years, prior to being released to her son in 1703. Retiring to the village where her son resided, she spent the rest of her life writing religious poetry, although she retained the support of several strong families within the French Court. All in all, she was as good a mystic as any other to have along for spiritual guidance on the river voyage.

Once again, Spear had either assembled in his own mind or been blessed with an extraordinary array of spirit friends. We are left, as we are throughout the Spear saga, with the paradoxical question: would these persons, having crossed into the afterlife, really care about what was happening in the temporal world, or, conversely, given their passion for humanity and faith, if they had awareness of temporal matters, how could they not care?

Guided by his spirit directors for the river voyage, Spear was on board the *Cleopatra*, a small steamship, when it set sail and served as the designated medium on board. Prior to departure, spirit-communications were received at Jamestown, Kiantone, and nearby Lander, PA. The apostles chose the individuals who were to accompany Spear on this trip. They were fourteen in number, including Mrs. Hinckley's baby. Beyond that, actual names were not listed, though the participants were described as members of the Harmonia constituency. In place of names, several of those signing on for the voyage were given titles by the apostles such as the *North Star*, the *Discerneress*, the *Constructor*, the *Pilot* [who may, in actuality, been just that, the man who steered the boat], the *Aggregationist*, the *Communicator*, and the *Recordess*.

Why the cryptic titles? Probably the best guess in answering that question has to do with where the group would be sailing. Their journey called for them to steam down the Allegheny River, into the Ohio River, and then the Mississippi River, with a final destination of *New Orleans*. They would be sailing along the actual borders of slave-holding and free states. They were committed abolitionists and it was not improbable that they might assist runaway slaves encountered along the way. To do so, in light of the Fugitive Slave Law, was a federal offense. They wanted, no doubt, to remain anonymous in the written record of the voyage.

Spear and his fellow mariners departed from *Oil City, PA* (Map 4) on December 2, 1859. Did they know that Cornplanter believed the oil found at this site had healing powers? There appears to be no answer to that question. Neither do records state what transportation they used to reach Oil City, approximately 60 miles southwest of Kiantone. It is possible that some of the travelers might have spent a few days with family and friends before departing. In that case, their journey to the rendezvous departure point may have been made overland by stagecoach. Others may have reached Oil Creek by flatboat or local steamer.

The spirits called this a "Columbusonian expedition" and the grandly stated purpose of the trip was to heal the wounds of the earth. That purpose, together with their departure date, could not have been more auspicious nor, to some American citizens, more inflammatory. The *December 2, 1859*, date was critical to their thoughts and emotions upon embarking on the river voyage. They were, right from the first day, trying to make a statement and they did. They embarked on the very same, well publicized date of *John Brown's* public execution.

John Brown "...was an extremist abolitionist who led the raid on Harper's Ferry and whose defeat, trial, and execution helped set the stage for the U.S. Civil War".[118] The South had long feared what would happen if the slaves decided to revolt against the tyranny of their masters. On October 16, 1859, Brown led a raid on the *Federal Arsenal* at Harpers Ferry, VA. The goal of the raid was to secure the arsenal's large number of muskets and rifles which Brown intended to place in the hands of slaves willing to join the revolt.

This was not Brown's first campaign against slavery. His far-flung abolition activities were well chronicled. Brown personally knew Frederick Douglass, the courageous free Black abolitionist. Douglass, indeed, spoke highly of Brown. For a time Brown lived in the *Adirondack Mountains* in Upstate New York, where he taught free Black farmers how to farm the area's rocky soil. In 1856, Brown, then living in Kansas, reportedly killed, some say, massacred, five pro-slavery settlers at *Patowatomie Creek*. This was in revenge against pro-slavery guerillas who burned *Lawrence, KS*, and killed many of its abolitionist citizens. Many Americans believed Brown was a brave and righteous man and there was even a Broadway play portraying him as a hero. Others saw him as an insurrectionist and a murderer.

Brown's raid at Harpers Ferry was put down, leading to his arrest, by a contingent of federal troops sent by *President James Buchanan*. Ironically, Buchanan specifically chose as the troops' leader none other than the distinguished Virginian, West Point graduate and career army officer, *Robert E. Lee*. Lee, of course, would later command the *Confederate Army of Northern Virginia*.

Brown's execution on December 2, 1859, was considered a tragedy by abolitionists and a victory for those who supported slavery. In a spirit message received by John Murray Spear on December 22, 1859, Brown is referred to as "the hero of '59".[119] In this same document, the spirits announce, regarding Brown, that "... it will be seen that there was method in his madness, that he had deliberately concocted a <u>scheme</u>, [*sic*, underlined in document] which <u>lives</u>, [*sic*, underline in document] and others may yet actualize what he in his earnestness and fidelity commenced". Spear and his group surely planned their departure for the exact day of Brown's execution. In mourning his death, they also were signaling their support of Brown's actions and beliefs.

Records do indicate that Spear and his fellow shipmates owned the steamship as a group. It is likely that, once again, Thaddeus Sheldon bankrolled the adventure. However, by this time, he had spent a considerable amount of his personal fortune supporting the spirit-gallivanting of John Murray Spear. This may have necessitated the pooling together of funds to purchase the steamship, which was named, *Cleopatra*.

One of the questions that occurred to me early in my research was the origin of this steamship. I mentioned that to a friend of mine, Ron Jacobs, a retired engineer who has a flare for computer research. Ron, who lives with his wife in their family home high above the Ohio River in Aurora, IN, went directly to work trying to answer my inquiry. Not surprisingly, *Cleopatra* was a name used for a variety of steamships, and most likely for a host of other types of vessels. I had doubts about whether we could identify a ship named *Cleopatra* that was the actual steamship used by the Kiantone group. But, after we looked at various websites, Ron came close to finding the right ship, even though hard evidence still eluded us.

Basically, Ron found three steamships named *Cleopatra* that were active in the United States during the time period of Spear's voyage. One was located in Connecticut and a second in California. While it would have been possible for either of those small steamships to sail the oceans and reach the Mississippi River and its tributaries, it seemed unlikely. There were other steamships named *Cleopatra* in the mid-1800s, but, with one exception, these were either lost (burned or shipwrecked) prior to 1859, or were built after 1860.

Ron's deductions about the various ships left us with one steamship named *Cleopatra* that fit the description. This ship would have been almost twenty years old by the time it was purchased by Spear and his compatriots. That might point to its being the right boat, as the price for a steamship of that age would have been reasonable, if not downright cheap.

This particular steamship, *Cleopatra,* was used for the infamous *Trail of Tears* (actually, there were several similarly named events) made by the *Choctaw* tribe in 1831, as they were moved from Mississippi to present-day southern Oklahoma.[120] This *Cleopatra,* described as a smaller ship, picked up tribal members at Vicksburg, MS and set about transporting them up the Red River to the Big Fork, eventually arriving at Monroe, LA. When they reached that settlement, another ship accompanying the *Cleopatra* became disabled, which necessitated the *Cleopatra's* ferrying multiple groups of Choctaw to Ecore a' Fabre (later, Camden, AR). The trips were plagued by poor planning, bad weather, and even a cholera outbreak, but it appears that the *Cleopatra* handled the challenge well. After that adventure, a ship named, *Cleopatra*, did not appear in Ron's research again until well after Spear's group completed their journey. Still, while is it plausible that the ship did serve in both settings, there is no concrete proof for this hypothesis.

In any event, Spear's group reached *Kittanning, PA* (Map 3) on December 4, 1859. They were not traveling at a fast speed, as the distance between Oil Creek and Kittanning is only approximately 63 miles. Still traveling at a leisurely pace, they reached *Pittsburgh*, about 42 miles further, on December 9. There they took time to visit some iron and steel factories, and Spear contemplated writing a series of papers on chattelism, serfdom, paid labor, and the relation the employer bears to the laborer.

By December 22, the *Cleopatra* moored near *Portsmouth, OH*, about 112 miles east of Cincinnati. Along the way, the steamship landed at different times on both the north and south sides of the river, that is, in *Pennsylvania, Virginia* (which at that time included today's *West Virginia*), *Ohio*, and *Kentucky*. It is quite possible that they took on fugitive slaves and set them across the river to continue their flight to freedom. If nothing else, for many of the travelers, it was their first eyewitness view of slavery.

We do not know where or how Spear and his group might have observed Christmas, a celebration that their Spiritualist beliefs would not necessarily have prohibited. But it is helpful to remember that the holiday, at that time, did not have the large complement of traditions associated with it that it has today. The holiday may simply have been observed with a special prayer, a toast, and a good meal.

On December 27, they moored again six miles east of Cincinnati, OH as the steamship berths in that city were almost always quite full. Although New Orleans was their ultimate destination, the *Cleopatra* and its Spiritualist travelers spent more time in Cincinnati than in any other town or city on their route. In fact, the city would remain their home for more than the next three months.

Although I tried to avoid using most spirit messages received by Spear and his colleagues, the séance transcription from December 27, 1859, must be cited here, as it set the course for Spear's work during the next several years. The document predicted the coming Civil War and implied that the *Union*, that is, the United States, would cease to exist as a whole.[121] Spear's thoughts for the next several years were driven by his belief in the coming demise of the United States as a nation and government. From this time, he saw himself and his movement as creating a new political and social reality that would, in his view, emerge out of the ashes of the American Civil War.

In Cincinnati, Spear and the others addressed both missionary concerns and practical needs. They recruited new members and added more berths to the *Cleopatra* to accommodate those who chose to join their river voyage. They also purchased a new propeller for the trip down the Mississippi River. This purchase might point to the ship being older, although the ever-changing river bottom was notorious for damaging the undersides of ships. All this necessitated their raising money to pay the bills. Subsequently, Spear and his voyagers held some séance sessions and lectures. This extended Cincinnati Spiritualist mission resulted in the identification of new financial supporters.

On January 19, 1860, while still at Cincinnati, Spear and his entourage received a spiritual communication that they were to bring world peace through a coming together of all nations, specifically the *United States, Russia, Great Britain, France, Germany* and *Japan*. Each nation was to govern itself without interfering in other nations' affairs, a kind of isolationism. The group also came to believe that they were to found a new universal religion that was to include a guarantee of women's rights.

Perhaps the most startling revelation recorded in Cincinnati was that the group, formerly known as Harmonia and the Domain, was to take on a new form and name, the *Sacred Order of Unionists*.[122] This new group (Appendix I) was intended to succeed Harmonia, the community that had been not quite dead after the 1858 convention, but surely on life support. A major goal of the Sacred Order of Unionists was revealed to be the establishment of cooperative international commerce, which, in addition to reshaping the earth's economy, would also provide Spear and his followers with a dependable financial foundation.

February 10, 1860, brought yet another new spiritually-transmitted plan to Spear and his colleagues. They now believed they were called to establish a new Spiritualist colony where they were to grow grapes for wine as a means of raising funds for their ventures. A farm was purchased at *Patriot, IN*, about 54 miles down river from Cincinnati. The farm consisted of 93 acres, with ten of those being in vineyards. They named it *Mount Alpheus*, after *Alpheus Cowles*, a local Spiritualist supporter.

Mount Alpheus was to be a partner community along with Kiantone. Plans were also made for establishing a third Spiritualist community in or near New Orleans, but that site never materialized. It seemed in the grand scheme (one of Spear's favorite words) of things that these three communities would play some kind of role after the approaching war between the North and South states. Perhaps the group entertained the idea that these colonies would be places where freed slaves could learn and practice farming, much like the Wilberforce Colony in Ontario. The exact purpose for them, however, remains somewhat cloudy.

Having moved from Western New York to Indiana in 2000, I found myself utterly shocked when I discovered that Spear and his followers had an Indiana connection. I learned this in the summer of 2004 while doing research at the *Smith Memorial Library* at *Chautauqua Institution*, the famous center for religion, education, music, and arts that was established in 1874. It was all I could do to keep from shouting out loud when I read about the Patriot Spiritualist colony. Oddly enough, my job in Indiana had taken me through that small river town several times before I ever knew anything about its history.

When I was back home in Indiana, I eventually contacted Janet Hendricks, the Switzerland County Historian, since that is the county where Patriot is located. She was helpful and said there might be some records at the county courthouse that would enable me to find the exact location of the Mount Alpheus colony. Then, fate intervened, and I lost my driver's license due to a vision impairment. Finally, in the summer of 2005, a good friend took a day and drove me down to the Ohio River Valley.

We met Mrs. Hendricks at the *Switzerland County Public Library's* local history room. Once again I explained to her what I was looking for. She was not sure what we might find. A local volunteer, Barry Brown, walked in, overheard our conversation, and then exclaimed, "Oh, you're looking for the Mount Alpheus file!" Well, that sounded absolutely great to me, but I was dumbfounded by what happened next. He retrieved the file, and to my astonishment, it contained many records, deeds, and letters related to the Mount

Alpheus colony. In addition, there were also letters sent to the Mount Alpheus colony members by persons like Thaddeus Sheldon and John Murray Spear.

I am sure that when I first saw those documents and realized their contents, I whooped out loud, just as I had almost done at the Chautauqua Institution library, not exactly the kind of behavior that is usually appreciated in libraries! However, my Switzerland County hosts were wonderful. Mrs. Hendricks quickly went to work reading the documents to me, while the friend who had driven me to Vevay started photocopying like crazy! What a wonderful historical find! With these documents in hand and with the help of Mr. Brown at the library, I was able to identify the plot number on an old county map for the land in Patriot where the Mount Alpheus colony was located. Actually, in the early 1860s, the property was just outside the southern boundary of Patriot, but when it was sold towards the end of that decade, it was incorporated into the town's limits.

Later that day, I had the opportunity to visit the *Life on the Ohio River History Museum* in Vevay. Typical of America's little roadside gems, it contains documents and artifacts depicting life and work along the Ohio River. I had hoped to learn if there were any ship records for Vevay, which is downstream from both Cincinnati and Patriot, indicating if the *Cleopatra* had moored there.

Well, I did not find any shipyard records in the museum, but I did find another wonderful Hoosier gem, a delightful older woman, Mrs. Erlene Leap. I briefly described for her the history I was researching. Then I sat spellbound as she described what life in Patriot, IN was like in the mid-1800s. Taking out a Switzerland County map (Map 6) she showed me how Patriot is located on the lower side of a giant u-shaped bend in the river that is surrounded on three sides by the Ohio River, and hence, by Kentucky. This

Indiana

Indianapolis

• Terre Haute

WABASH RIVER

Patriot •

↳ Site of
Mount
Alpheus
colony

• Evansville

OHIO RIVER

Indiana

Map 6

meant, according to Mrs. Leap, that runaway slaves frequently approached the little river town from three sides, often with fugitive slave hunters in close pursuit. She told me about her daughter's home, an old house from that time period. Underneath the living room rug was a secret trap door where runaway slaves could quickly escape to the basement if slave hunters suddenly appeared at the front door.

This runaway slave activity, as described by Mrs. Leap, corresponds with a Mount Alpheus document located at the library in Vevay. Previously, someone (no name given) had typed a transcription of an agreement made on February 12, 1862, between *W. B. Johnson* and *John Orvis*, a Spiritualist from Cincinnati and a business partner with John Murray Spear. Orvis signed the document as an agent for Thaddeus Sheldon, who, in addition to his Randolph, NY ventures, had business concerns in Cincinnati and was engaged in Spiritualist activities in that area, too. Sheldon, evidently, was a financial backer for the Mount Alpheus colony and may, in fact, have been the only financial supporter. The document detailed how the vineyard and fruit orchard work was to be done at Mount Alpheus. It also explicitly stated that Mr. Johnson was to maintain utmost privacy regarding activities that took place on the estate.

The said Mr. Johnson will study to be quiet, orderly & exemplary in all the conduct while on or about the estate and he will not invite non residents upon the estate, without having first obtained the counsel of the Presiding Matron of the estate and it will be expected, that he will not report to the neighborhood or to non residents any information of the business or plans of the residents or of the proprietor in so far as he may know them and he is strictly prohibited the contraction of any debt in behalf of the estate or its proprietor and it will be expected that he will so deport himself, towards the residents of the place and the people of the neighborhood as so promote harmony among the former and good feeling on the part of the latter – [sic, dash punctuation mark in original document][123]

This document, I think, points to the great possibility of runaway slave activity on the Mount Alpheus property, and the possibility of Free Love activities as well. It may only have been Patriot, IN, but for Spear and colleagues, it was *terra incognita* and worthy of utmost caution.

One of Mrs. Leap's observations was uniquely chilling. President Abraham Lincoln announced the Emancipation Proclamation on September 22, 1862, and it became effective on January 1, 1863. I asked Mrs. Leap if the proclamation precipitated a sudden end to the pursuit of the newly-freed slaves traveling to the North. With a rueful and sad look, she shook her head, indicating, "No". Then, she told me that after the proclamation, the hunters still pursued the freed slaves, but just shot them dead where they found them. She said folks walking in the woods and fields in the hills above the town frequently came across these murdered former slaves, left to rot where they dropped.

Still later that afternoon, my friend and I found the exact spot in Patriot where the colony had been located. We were able to gain access to the Mount Alpheus property that directly fronts the Ohio River. It is amazing that the river in that section looks remarkably like Chautauqua Lake as viewed from Greenhurst or the area near the Lakewood Rod and Gun Club. This is because the river at that location is about two or three football fields wide and stretches about a half mile in either direction. I wondered if Spear and his group noticed the similarities.

The property was for sale by the owner, so I wrote down the phone number and spoke to the woman the next day. It turned out that she and her husband had just recently moved into the house next door and were actually home the previous day. I asked her if she knew about the property's history and she replied that she knew about the runaway slave traffic. But, she was amazed when I outlined the Mount Alpheus saga to her.

Everything I had learned about Patriot and Mount Alpheus was helpful as I looked at the scant written record of the *Cleopatra* and its crew on the remainder of their voyage to New Orleans. There is no doubt that they developed a very complete understanding of the dangers faced by runaway slaves and the peril experienced by those who might help them, let alone those who were committed abolitionists. No doubt, Spear and his fellow voyagers were careful to put very little of all this down in their journals. Daniel Gano, the Cincinnati Spiritualist mentioned earlier, wrote a letter of reference for Spear on March 5, 1860, probably believing that Spear would soon be on his way down the river. But, by late March, the *Cleopatra* and its passengers were still in Cincinnati. It is very possible that, by that time, they had developed cold feet for the task to which they believed they were called. Or, they could just have been waiting for the spring snowmelt to raise the river level, an occurrence that happened frequently before the elaborate system of dams was built on the river.

At last, they departed Cincinnati, bound for New Orleans and ports beyond. The steamship made a short stop in *Memphis, TN.* The *Sheldon Papers* included a reference to the group thinking that Memphis could become a great Spiritualist center. The *Cleopatra,* according to their records, arrived in New Orleans by May 5, 1860. On that day, Spear dictated a lengthy séance set of instructions about what the group was supposed to accomplish in Cuba.[124] What is striking about this document is that it included a vast array of proposed activities that would have taken many months, if not longer, to accomplish. These included studying health issues, customs, manners, and habits of the Cuban people, as well as cataloging fruits, and discerning what was important to learn from Cuba's monasteries and convents. They were also told that in Cuba, they were to write many papers about theology and commerce.

Another instruction proved, at least to me, to be quite fascinating. In addition to writing the papers cited, in Cuba Spear's group was to perform an extensive analysis of the voyagers' minds to determine to what degree their thinking had been *foreignized*. Surely this May 5, 1860, document signals Spear's intention to sail all the way to Cuba including, as stated in the document, to the "W.L.," that is, the *Western Leeward Islands*, including *St. Thomas, St. Martin*, and *St. John*.

Still, I was somewhat confounded by their desire to sail to Cuba until a retired history teacher told me that one of the goals of the Southern states prior to the Civil War was to have Cuba become part of the United States and enter as a slave state. This would have given the Southern cause two additional votes in the United States Senate and proportional votes in the House of Representatives. Spear and others in his group surely knew about the South's goal, so their visit would have been an opportunity for them to convince Cubans of the validity of the abolitionist sentiment.

The reality, however, was that Spear, by all accounts, never got far beyond New Orleans. Early in the voyage, Spear and his fellow travelers had announced their intentions to spread their Spiritualist version of peace to *Florida, Texas*, and to *Cuba*. There is some evidence that the group steamed 90 miles south of New Orleans to the mouth of the Mississippi River and then on to *Mobile, AL*, but that may have been just a few days excursion. Perhaps, that was also when they realized that the *Cleopatra* was not suitable for an ocean voyage. Thus, New Orleans, in most respects, was the actual culminating destination of the river voyage.

However, this in no way denigrates what Spear and his crew accomplished. Today, there is a tendency to think of New Orleans, sadly, as a badly damaged tourist attraction. But, in the mid-19th Century, New Orleans was the central port for both ocean-going and riverboat traffic. The waters of many rivers, including the Allegheny, the Ohio, the Yellowstone, the Missouri, the Cumberland, the Arkansas, the Red, and the Mississippi, plus all the many, many smaller rivers and creeks that constituted their tributaries flowed through New Orleans. Mail, freight, passengers, and banking were all connected to New Orleans via this vast interstate water system. Ships from around the world docked in New Orleans. If someone had a message to share, then New Orleans was the place to take it!

Spear and his group probably knew something about the culture of mid-19th Century New Orleans because Thaddeus Sheldon had conducted river raft trade with businesses in that city. Still, we can only imagine how strange and exotic New Orleans must have seemed to these New England and upper Midwest folks. If one, previously, thought that the Kiantone Valley could be or should be the spiritual center of the earth, then arriving in New Orleans would have been quite a shock! New Orleans was a mixed culture of past, present, and future death, all swirling together in a spiritual eddy. Already, its residents had learned to bury their dead in the city's unique above-ground graves, a practice they thought impeded the spread of disease, but really was just better suited for the city's high water table. Graves were marked by stone mausoleums, some modest in appearance, and others lavishly constructed. New Orleans, underneath its veneer of gaiety, had a morbid countenance. *Necromancy*, a form of divination through the deceased, was practiced throughout the city. These realities helped define the city's culture, which, indeed, had seen more than its share of death since its earliest settlement, with frequent epidemics, including yellow fever.

Moreover, *psychics* had long practiced their craft in New Orleans and *Voodoo*, a mixture of African cults and Roman Catholicism, was practiced by the city's West Indies Black population. To add to the mix, the European heritage population faithfully retained their *Roman Catholic* religious rites and rituals. Add in a few *Methodists, Anglicans, Presbyterians*, and an occasional *Baptist*, and the city was a virtual stew of religious ingredients.

The ethnic diversity of persons living in New Orleans must have been a conundrum for Spear's contingent. In addition to *English, French, Spanish*, and *German* people, the *Irish* had recently arrived. Upper class New Orleans businesspeople viewed the Irish as worthless, and in a slave-driven economy that was lower than low. This view was put into practice with the Irish being hired as ditch-diggers for canal projects, with a resulting horrific death rate from this work. *Mulattos* (half-Black), *quadroons* (one-quarter Black), and all sorts of persons with some African descent were part of the city's social fabric, while slaves were called *Blacks* and free persons of color were called *Colored*. In New Orleans, Spear and the other river voyagers were confronted face-to-face with the terrible reality of slavery. The New Orleans notorious slave market, which, by 1850, had become the largest slave market in the United States, probably both appalled and sickened these dedicated abolitionists.

Still, there was more to the ethnic stew called New Orleans. *Creoles*, native-born New Orleans residents of Spanish and French heritage, also played a dominant role in the city's social structure. The river voyagers arrived after *Mardi Gras* (begun in 1837), *Lent*, and

Easter, so late spring festivities and soirees with varying ethnic flavors must have been in high gear.

Spear's group undoubtedly suffered severe *culture shock* when they reached the lower Mississippi River. Even knowing that they would not write anything about any assistance they might have given to runaway slaves, the record of what they actually accomplished in both Memphis and New Orleans is sparse, to say the least. One cannot overlook the absence of such information, an observation I pondered for months. In late 2005, I obtained a copy of Emma Hardinge's book, *Modern American Spiritualism: A Twenty Years' Record of the Communion Between Earth and the World of the Spirits*. In several chapters describing the spread of Spiritualism into the South, Mrs. Hardinge, an Englishwoman who resided for long periods in the United States, provided valuable clues as to the mystery regarding Spear's venture into the Deep South.

In particular, Mrs. Hardinge cites her own visit to Memphis in 1859, where she was invited to give a lecture on Spiritualism as a fund-raiser for an orphanage. Several rowdy persons showed up, and there was even a threat of lynching Mrs. Hardinge and her supporters. The next day, as she gave a lecture at a Sunday service, a large stone was thrown at her through a window, shattering the window panes, but falling harmlessly at her feet. A letter subsequently sent to the Memphis *Inquirer* newspaper indicated that the transgression Mrs. Hardinge had committed was to present Spiritualism, not as a British Spiritualist, but as a New England abolitionist. That is, her speech had somehow meddled in the tawdry affairs of slavery, rather than simply addressing Spiritualism. Mrs. Hardinge's 1859 visit to Memphis was prior to Spear's 1860 visit. No doubt, he was aware of the dangers faced by New England abolitionists when traveling and speaking in the Southern states.

Spiritualism had been practiced in New Orleans for several years leading up to the Civil war, with Whites, as well as Blacks and Creoles, serving as mediums. In the book cited above, Mrs. Hardinge noted that she visited New Orleans in December 1859, just as Spear's river voyage was beginning. She stayed in the home of a wealthy businessman and enjoyed the pleasures of a festive English-style *Yuletide*. Following the New Year's festivities, Mrs. Hardinge gave a series of lectures about Spiritualism and was well received. She states in her book that Spiritualism had, by this time, taken a firm hold in New Orleans, and that late 1859, saw several well-known mediums descending upon the city, each being met with enthusiasm and support.

Still, Mrs. Hardinge rightly notes the difficulties that Spiritualism proposed for antebellum Southerners, since it was a belief system thought to be thoroughly democratic in nature and without prejudice to race or class. That some Southerners embrace Spiritualism, but many did not, created tension in a region already stretched like a violin string wound far too tightly.

What then, can we make of Spear's visit to New Orleans on the steamer *Cleopatra*, with his entourage of other Spiritualist and abolitionist-minded folks? My own hunch is that several factors contributed to there being very little written record about his visit to the *Crescent City*, as New Orleans is often called. First, he may well have become aware of the challenge Spiritualism was presenting to the pro-slavery proponents of the South and their occasional violent reaction to intruding New England abolitionists. Second, the wave of Spiritualists who had visited the city in the previous months may have worn out the welcome mat. Those who came before Spear may have so successfully presented Spiritualism that Spear appeared as the proverbial "Johnny come lately". Thus, the New Orleans folks may have simply moved on to the next great theme of the day, that is, the impending fracture in the Union.

Finally, Spear and his colleagues were dangerously low on funds. Spear had to tap into his personal savings to keep the mission afloat while the entire group did some frantic fund-raising. Faced with financial disaster, in the midst of an impending national crisis, and with a long way to go before they reached home again, the group simply skedaddled back to Cincinnati as quickly as possible. Whether they made the trip by river or by train we simply do not know, nor do we know what happened to the steamship, *Cleopatra*.

To be perfectly honest, I had and still have reservations about Spear's claim that they ever reached New Orleans and Mobile. Granted, they had plenty of time to sail the river that far. I checked out sailing distances and times along the Ohio and Mississippi rivers as noted in Mark Twain's classic, *Life on the Mississippi*. Ron Jacobs did the same on various Internet sites There was more than enough time between early May and late June 1860 to sail from Cincinnati to New Orleans and back again, even for a small steamship.

Wishing to examine this question further, I decided to visit New Orleans myself and see if I could find any documentation about the *Cleopatra*. Previously, I had visited the city twice on business, but in early 2005, I returned for a combination vacation and research trip. In retrospect, given the impact of *Hurricane Katrina*, I am in awe regarding the timing of my visit. Maybe it was coincidence, maybe it was spirit-led, or maybe it was just fate. In any event, I had a wonderful opportunity to linger in the *French Quarter* as well as explore other New Orleans neighborhoods that now are simply gone, perhaps forever.

After inquiry in New Orleans, I discovered that *The Williams Research Center, The Historic New Orleans Collection*, had microfilm copies of the *Daily Crescent*, a New Orleans newspaper that carried

19th Century reports of daily steamship arrivals and departures. I checked these reports for the time period from the first half of 1860, but found no mention of the *Cleopatra*. Ron Jacobs also had the opportunity to the visit New Orleans a few months later. He, too, searched the records, but found nothing. Reviewing my research notes, one of the most humorous comments either of us encountered was made by a New Orleans history center volunteer. When I told him about John Murray Spear and his river voyage for peace in 1859-1860, the man replied, "He's lucky he was not shot!"

Another friend suggested, since I knew the *Cleopatra* had reached Patriot, IN, that I check the *Louisville, KY* canal and ship locks records to see if the steamship had made it that far down the Ohio River. The folks at the *United States Army Corps of Engineers* were helpful and put me in touch with a retired corps historian, Charles Parrish. Alas, he told me that he understood precisely what I was looking for, but that those documents had been lost for some time. He feared they might never be found or that they might have been destroyed. Remembering that the *Sheldon Papers* turned up in someone's attic, approximately 73 years after Sheldon's death, all I can say is that it behooves everyone to always be on the lookout when cleaning out old papers and documents.

So ends the tale of the river voyage. By July 1, 1860, Spear and his fellow travelers had returned to Cincinnati. On that day, Spear wrote a letter[125] to Sheldon from nearby Vine Hill about the river voyage, including the names of some contacts made in New Orleans. The letter, however, is far more about the future, particularly the newly-established Sacred Order of Unionists, than about the river expedition. Obviously, by this time, Spear was looking to the future, not the past. The results of the voyage were certainly mixed. Spear and his followers had made a feeble attempt at creating world peace. Overall, despite their desire to make a strong statement on behalf of Spiritualism, their faith had been sorely tested and the voyage did not amount to much.

Of singular importance was the revelation received in route, namely that the old days of their Spiritualist community, solely focused on the harmonial Domain at Kiantone, was coming to an end. They were now responsible for both maintaining the Kiantone property and the new colony at Patriot. They were also called to found a new organization, the Sacred Order of Unionists, which would operate both on behalf of the spirits as well as for business and fund-raising purposes.

Still, they had tried. The river voyage and their attempt at peace-making, made when a cruel era was dawning in America, was the only attempt of its kind in that day. Sadly, it did not bring peace to the nation.

Even so, it all still leaves me humming about a yellow submarine.

CHAPTER 10

THE CIVIL WAR YEARS AND THEREAFTER
EVERYTHING CHANGED

What is it that makes the Kiantone saga so intriguing? The land and beautiful geographic location certainly are contributing factors. However, there are many other beautiful and distinctive places. What makes Kiantone unique, I think, is its extraordinary human story. Viewed as a whole, this human story is marked by a sense of the mystical, the hard-working practical, and, in the case of the Harmonia experiment, the sometimes spiritual coupled with the sometimes comical. In the 1860s, however, the tragedy of the Civil War struck this tiny place, even as it did the entire nation. And with this war, everything changed.

HAMLET OF KIANTONE

The first settlers and their descendants continued to labor faithfully throughout the middle years of the 1800s. The days of frontier destitution passed, and the community moved from mere survival to an era of prosperity. Attention now turned to matters of community organization. The first town meeting was held on February 21, 1854. This resulted in the election of town officials including a *supervisor* (Ezbai Kidder), *town clerk* (Levant B. Brown), *town superintendent of schools* (Francis M. Alvord), *tax collector* (Stephan Norton) and several persons who served variously as *assessors, inspectors of elections, highway commissioners, overseers of the poor, justices of the peace*, and *constables*. With multiple persons serving in the latter categories, it appears that each man attending the meeting was awarded some type of title and responsibility. Similar elections took place regularly thereafter.

During the 1860s, the rumblings of a nation ever more divided over the issue of slavery became thunderous and inescapable. Despite this approaching storm, the hamlet of Kiantone continued to prosper and develop. The construction and improvement of roads and bridges was a continual concern, with residents contributing annually to a $150 fund designated for this work. Not all citizens were able to pay in cash, so labor was accepted as an in-kind contribution to the fund. One-room school houses were erected. A post office took the new town name on April 4, 1855. It remained the town's only post office until it was discontinued in 1900. Its eventual demise was related to the size of the community. The population always remained small, and the town was geographically the smallest in Chautauqua County.

In the 1850s, John Murray Spear, the ardent abolitionist, had come to the nearby wooded valley. The locals likely overlooked his abolitionist message as they watched from afar the other antics and goings-on that Spear and his fellow Spiritualists practiced. In the 1860s, the noble and just abolition cause would exact a terrible price from Kiantone's families, as it did from thousands of families across the nation. The spine of slavery would be broken, but so would the hearts of families and friends throughout the land.

One early settler, James Hall, as noted in Chapter 3, came to Kiantone in 1812. Life was tenuous on the frontier in those early days. Hall, as previously noted, married not just one, but three of Ebenezer Cheney's daughters. This unusual series of unions came about because each wife died, therefore, freeing Hall to marry the next available sister. Thus, Hall fathered six children with the first and third Cheney wives. James and Maria Hall's son, *James Hall*, fought in the Civil War and died at the *Battle of Malvern Hill*.

Malvern Hill was the final battle of the *Seven Days' Battles* fought on June 25 to July 1, 1862. That spring, Union forces had already won the *Battle of Shiloh (Pittsburgh Landing)*, but at a deadly cost to both sides. New Orleans had fallen to Union Naval forces led by Admiral David G. Farragut. In the east, a Confederate general, Thomas J. Jackson, known by this time as *Stonewall* Jackson, kept a ferocious hold on the Shenandoah Valley. Meanwhile, the Union Army of the Potomac, directed by General George B. McClellan, sought to encircle Richmond, VA in a stranglehold, believing that such a feat would surely end the war quickly.

On the last day of the fight for Richmond, the Confederate capital, Union forces nearing the James River held the high ground on Malvern Hill, thought to be impregnable. The fighting was fierce, with 5,300 Confederate casualties and 3,200 Union casualties. Despite their overwhelming losses, the Confederates did not give an inch. Although the Union Army also remained steadfast, McClellan chose not to pursue General Robert E. Lee's beleaguered troops. Rather, McClellan retreated with his troops to Fort Harrison and the safety of the James River where his forces could be protected by Union gunboats. It was almost a miracle that the South, under Lee's direction, barely managed to win the Seven Days' Battles. The loss of any Civil War soldier was disheartening for the man's family. But the fact that James Hall's death came as the result of a battle that did little to advance the Union cause, must have been doubly painful for his family and his Kiantone friends and neighbors.

I offer a lengthy description of the Battle of Malvern Hill to illustrate the kind of information that heart-broken family members yearned for regarding their loved one's death. The place and date of death offered little information. In the Civil War, as in all wars, surviving parents, siblings, and spouses always wanted a clear vision of the circumstances of their fallen soldiers, so they could rightly place their family's patriotic sacrifice in a personal perspective of honor. No doubt, the citizens of Kiantone, their lives changed forever by Civil War casualties, yearned for such information.

The Seven Days' Battles not only resulted in a Union retreat, but also drove the Union away from a staging point from which they could capture the Confederate capital at Richmond. It also revealed that Lee, previously thought by many in the South to be just a doddering old warrior, was really the fierce commander they so badly needed if the South was to be victorious. Thus, the Seven Days' Battles set the stage for bloody and deadly consequences that would persist for three more terrible years.

Another early settler, Ebenezer Chapin, settled in southeast Kiantone in 1830. Of his seven children, one, Sylvester, became a Union soldier. *Sylvester Chapin* was wounded in early 1865, probably in the taking of the Confederate seaport once protected by the fortifications at the Cape Fear River mouth, but now fallen to the Union forces. Sylvester's wound was not severe. He was deemed strong enough to work at a Union hospital in Wilmington, NC. Civil War hospitals were notoriously dangerous breeding grounds for illnesses, including typhoid, smallpox, and dysentery. Sylvester escaped death in battle, but, like many Civil War soldiers, he contracted disease and died far from home.

William Martin was among Kiantone's earliest settlers. He fathered nine children, six sons and three daughters. Seven of his children lived to adulthood, and one of Martin's sons, Isaac, had two daughter and seven sons. Three of Isaac's sons took active roles in the Civil War. Notably, *Edgar Martin* fought in several battles, including the *Battle of Williamsburg*.

As often happened in the early years of the Civil War, Williamsburg, the first battle of the 1862 *Peninsula Campaign*, was an opportunity lost. The Confederate forces, numbering 32,000, were withdrawing from Yorktown. The Union forces were strong, numbering 41,000. Engaging and repulsing the Southern troops, the Federals, nevertheless, then allowed them to escape. Many battles would follow and it is easy to think of Edgar ruefully wishing the job had been completed in 1862.

Isaac Martin's second son, *Emery Martin*, served as an assistant in a hospital and apparently finished the war unharmed. A third son, *Albert Martin*, saw duty in the *Battle of Fort Fisher* at the mouth of the Cape Fear River in North Carolina. This battle took place on January 13, 1865 and ended with a Union victry. It was significant because Fort Fisher, made of dirt and sand, guarded General Lee's last open seaport, a vital supply port for the Confederate troops who were dug in at Petersburgh, VA. When the war ended in April 1865, Emery must have brought home to Kiantone a sense of having helped write the final chapter of the terrible conflict. It appears that all three Martin brothers survived the war. One can only imagine what tales they had to tell around the cracker barrel back in Kiantone at the general store when the war was over!

Other early settlers, whose children had roots in Kiantone but moved westward, also had heirs who both served and died in the Civil War. Andrew W. Young's *History of Chautauqua County, New York: From Its First Settlement to Present Time* (1875) provides lengthy family histories of early settlers and their families. An account about William Sears, after whom Kiantone was first named Searsville, notes that one of Sears' grandsons fought and died in the southwestern Civil War theater, possibly under the command of General Ulysses

S. Grant. Sears son, *Clinton W. Martin,* became a preacher in Ohio, near Cincinnati, after formal training at *Yale College* and *Wesleyan University.* This son served as a chaplain with the Union Army. During the *Siege of Vicksburg* (May 18 to July 4, 1863) he became ill, returned home, presumably to either Cincinnati or Kiantone, and died of illness in 1863. Whether his death occurred in Ohio or New York, it was surely noted and mourned by neighbors who remembered the early days of Searsville. It is also possible that the grandson who died in the Civil War was Clinton Sear's son. This poignant scenario could be an interesting project for someone wanting to do some genealogical research.

Ironically, the Civil War years marked a time of continued community development in Kiantone. Meanwhile, many sacrifices were made by the hamlet's soldiers who lost their lives in the conflict and those battle-scarred veterans who returned from the bloody fields. The Civil War changed many families forever, but it also reunited the nation and ended slavery. The ensuing assassination of President Abraham Lincoln shook the nation's foundations even as the *Reconstruction Era* challenged its political and moral base. Like so many small towns and city neighborhoods across the United States, Kiantone's citizens discovered that everything had changed.

KIANTONE'S SPIRITUAL LANDSCAPE

It seems probable that Kiantone's citizens were aware of how Spiritualism had its beginnings in Hydesville with the Fox sisters in 1848. They surely knew of Harmonia's activities taking place along the banks of the Kiantone Creek. However, it also appears that most of the hamlet's citizens did not choose the Spiritualist path.

In 1845, several years prior to John Murray Spear's coming to Kiantone, a group of Universalists built a meeting house. This group grew stronger over the next several years. Their history is rather interesting, in terms of ecclesiastical language, as they first formed a church on November 26, 1853, and then the first *Christian Society of Universalists* in Carroll on December 30, 1853. Initially, the society contained about twenty-five members. None of the founders' names listed reflect those who were involved in Harmonia, except for Oliver G. Chase, who was the father of Oliver F. Chase and the brother of John Chase (see Chapter 8). It is likely that Oliver G. Chase became acquainted with John Murray Spear through his brother, John Chase, and that is how Oliver F. Chase came to do some work for the Harmonia group.

The Congregational congregation was originally founded in 1815, as the *First Church of Ellicott*, as the hamlet was then located in the Town of Ellicott. In 1825, it became the *Congregational Church of Carroll*, since the hamlet was now part of that town. In 1830, a meeting-house was built on a site given to the society by Mrs. Ruby (Cheney) Sears, eldest daughter of Ebenezer Cheney and wife of William Sears, the first tavern owner. In 1853, the church again changed its name to reflect the name of the town in which it was now located. Today, the *Kiantone Congregational Church*, a small, rural congregation, is still active, while the Universalist congregation long ago ceased to exist.

Also active in the surrounding towns and settlements during this time were other Christian groups, including the Methodists, Baptists, and Presbyterians. Surely, the members and pastors of these congregations had much to say about the Spiritualist activities of the Harmonia community. Fact may often have been difficult to separate from fiction, as rumors spread about the unusual events that from time to time took place along the banks of the Kiantone Creek. We can only speculate how these various Christian groups responded to what they knew or thought they knew.

After its beginnings in Hydesville in 1848, Spiritualism quickly began to spread throughout the United States and elsewhere. There is little doubt that some local pastors taught lessons and preached sermons about the Biblical texts which they understood to prohibit Spiritualist activities. There is, actually, a significant list of such texts in the *Bible*, particularly in the *Old Testament*. For example, Deuteronomy 18:10-11 and similar teachings in Leviticus, including Leviticus 19:31, prohibit tolerance of those who would seek to communicate with the dead. Leviticus 20:6 boldly states that God will cut off from their own people those who seek the assistance of mediums. Finally, Leviticus 20:27 teaches that mediums should be stoned; thus creating, at least to my 21st Century mind and heart, a good argument for religious freedom and tolerance!

These ideas and teachings are echoed throughout the Old Testament. However, the *New Testament* writings are somewhat different from those of the Old Testament in that they do not contain as many strident teachings against consulting with mediums. Still, it should be assumed that New Testament Christians, at least those who had previously worshipped as Jews, would already know the Old Testament teachings. Moreover, those who recorded and wrote the new covenant firmly believed that Jesus the Christ had produced the most significant revelation of God. Thus, believers were encouraged to look only to the Risen Christ for revelation of those things believed, but, yet, unseen.

As previously noted, it does not appear that large numbers of Kiantone's local citizens affiliated with the Harmonia community. The hamlet's Unitarians may well have stayed away because John Murray Spear was no longer a sanctioned Unitarian pastor, due to his Spiritualist activities. The Congregationalists and others, no doubt, heard strong sermons vilifying the Domain. It should be noted that many Spiritualists, however, did value (and continue to value today) the Bible and its teachings and saw them in the light of their own understandings. There is no record that tells of Spiritualists who might have attempted to explain to Kiantone's citizens that, from their perspective, being a Spiritualist did not necessarily preclude being a Christian. My hunch, however, is that those kinds of conversations did occur.

There is another possible reason that Kiantone's local community did not sign on with the Spiritualist camp. They may simply have failed to see in Harmonia's witness evidence of good *fruit*, that is, faith connected to acts of compassion and *agape* (Grk.), the latter being love in the sense of general love of humanity. The Christians may have come to understand that traditional Christian beliefs, based on their understandings of the Bible, appeared to bear more blessed fruit than did the Spiritualist beliefs and actions. That is my best hunch, but the darker side of mid-1800s Christian evangelical teachings probably points to the clergy simply convincing their parishioners that, if they believed in Spiritualism, they would go to hell. This was not, afterall, the era of ecumenical appreciation for various expressions of Christianity.

Finally, there is almost no doubt that the hamlet's social mores and values simply rejected Harmonia's combination of Spiritualism with Free Love. Thus, if one wanted to remain a member of the tiny hamlet's respectable community, one did not cross either the theological or the sociological line. No doubt, Kiantone's community leaders breathed a sigh of relief as they witnessed the demise of the Domain in the 1860s and viewed it as a change for the better.

HARMONIA (THE DOMAIN) COMES TO AN END

Harmonia's end came with the proverbial whimper and not with a roar. Various contributing factors brought on the experiment's demise.

Certainly, decreasing financial support played a significant role. By the early 1860s, Thaddeus Sheldon, the principal underwriter, had sunk most of his fortune into the Domain as well as many civic projects and churches in Randolph. In May 1860, Alpheus Cowles represented the group in the purchase of the Mount Alpheus property in Patriot, IN. This second colony was never very prosperous and quickly became a drain on everyone's pocketbook.

On January 1, 1861, John Murray Spear wrote a New Year's address that was circulated to various parties. The tone of the address was hopeful. Citing other leaders in the socialist movement, such as *Robert Owen* and *Emanuel Swedenborg*, Spear announced that new buildings would rise at Kiantone to replace the temporary structures.[126] That same day, Spear also wrote a prayer imploring that the sick would come to Kiantone for healing.[127] This supplication was, perhaps, as much for the healing of the sick as for the revenue the healings might generate to help maintain the Domain's property and facilities.

In the midst of such hope, the very structure and organization of Harmonia was changing. Also on January 1, 1861, Spear and Sheldon agreed to lease the Domain's lands in Kiantone to Horace Fenton, most likely for agricultural purposes. This transaction included the understanding that Fenton would return it to them whenever the Association of Beneficients asked for it.[128]

More changes continued throughout the year. Mary Gardner agreed to take over supervision of Kiantone on August 1, 1861.[129] She was entrusted with sole authority over the Domain and was given the title, *Matron of the Home Department*. In a document, dated January 1, 1861, Spear had written about the importance of a woman being placed in such a position.[130]

In 1862, Spear persisted in hoping that the two colonies would have a bright future. On May 1, 1862, he unveiled a five-year financial plan for both Harmonia and Mount Alpheus.[131] But, by this time, Spear was probably in denial of the truth. A June 5, 1862, letter from *C. F. Doone*, one of the Patriot colony's leaders, to Thaddeus Sheldon indicated that finances at Mount Alpheus were faring poorly.[132] Additional reports indicated a steady decline in both ventures and their eventual demise during the Civil War years.

When an institution is unraveling, as Harmonia was in the 1860s, it is often difficult to point to one particular reason for the institution's decline. Such may be the case for Harmonia. Both the wider faith community, as well as the evolving Spiritualist denomination, increasingly took a dim view of Harmonia's involvement with Free Love and its new organizational plan, the Sacred Order of Unionists. It did not help matters that the Sacred Order was presented as a kind of *secret society.*

In May 1862, a group of Spiritualist leaders assembled a court of inquiry, including a judge and jury, at *Lyceum Hall* in Boston. This was the *first ever judicial body called together in Spiritualist history.* The purpose of the court of inquiry was to examine what had taken place at Kiantone and, more specifically, the ministry of John Murray Spear. The basic charges were "immoral practices, teachings, and tendencies".[133]

In her description of the inquiry, Mrs. Hardinge described the defense as just that, defensive. Evidently, those accused proclaimed that they were pure of heart and mind, and, therefore, anything they did was pure. This defense did not win the day.

Moreover, Mrs. Hardinge appeared to indicate in her account of the trial that there was a conscious effort on behalf of the Boston Spiritualists to keep the most sensational aspects of Kiantone's Harmonia out of the Boston press. A lasting outcome of the trial was the codifying of acceptable Spiritualist practices. These were recorded in a document entitled, *Declaration of Principles of the Ly-*

ceum Church. This document was widely printed and distributed. The overall result, as Mrs. Hardinge explained, was that the Harmonia leaders simply and "... silently returned to the well-beaten paths of ordinary life, in which they have doubtless found both safety and usefulness".[134] This was her polite way of saying that they just faded away.

Mrs. Hardinge's comments were not always so polite. Consider the following quotation:

By temporarily fastening an obnoxious reputation upon the noble cause of Spiritualism, the "Kiantone Movement" called forth discussions and eliminated questions of the highest import, which have been of incalculable benefit, and have ended in the sifting process which sooner or later was essential to free Spiritualism from all other claims and pretensions than the sublime purposes of proving the soul's immortality, the unity of spirit, and individual responsibility. All other side issues are fungi springing up from the corruption of undeveloped natures, and, like the morals of Kiantone, must ultimately be shaken off from the divine body, on which they are simple excrescence.[135]

Of one thing I am sure. I would not want to have Mrs. Hardinge mad at me!

Thaddeus Sheldon died, on July 17, 1868, at age fifty. He had been plagued by thoughts of death for years, no doubt augmented by the 1849 cholera epidemic and the consumption he battled every winter during the last years of his life. In retrospect, it is likely that his fixation on death lead to his commitment to Spiritualism. Sheldon's fortune, once immense, was gone by 1862. He had exhausted it by supporting the many whims and schemes of John Murray Spear. Despite his financial insolvency, Sheldon remained an ardent supporter of John Murray Spear until his last breath.

Eventually, John Sterling purchased the Harmonia property and gave it in trust to the Kiantone Board of Trustees for "educational and healing purposes".[136] They built a school on it, but abandoned it within three years for unknown reasons, though we may speculate that the property was viewed by Kiantone residents as somewhat tainted. In the 1880s, after Sterling died, the land then reverted to Sterling's heirs. They placed it in the hands of a Jamestown attorney, *Edward R. Bootey*, who sold it for cattle grazing land. Eventually, it passed into the hands of a member of the Cheney family. In the mid-20th Century a family campground called *Hidden Valley* was established along Kiantone Creek. It would be, perhaps, interesting to do a careful study of the various creek-side properties related to the Harmonia story at the *Chautauqua County Courthouse* in Mayville.

Local Kiantone farmers tore down the last of the Domain's octagon cottages for firewood in 1907. Prior to 1900, an eccentric elderly woman, *Ann Head*, spent summers in it. Could this have been the young woman from Cattaraugus who spoke so radically at the 1858 convention? It could be worth the effort of a genealogist to explore the question of Head's identity.

JOHN MURRAY SPEAR

John Murray Spear was no longer a young man. Born in 1804, he was in his late fifties by the time things started to unravel at Kiantone. Nevertheless, Spear's strong sense of both call and destiny propelled him into the next chapter of his life. Once again, it is helpful to look at Hardinge's narrative about the Spiritualist trial that found Harmonia to be, ironically, in disharmony with the basic tenants of Spiritualism, as well as her veiled description of John Murray Spear and similar leaders:

>...*the vagaries of fanatics, or one-idea reformers, who, speculating on the credulity of their fellow mortals, planned schemes for elevating themselves into positions of leadership.* [137]

Even before the 1862 trial and as far back as 1860, Spear was still tied to the visions of what could be, both at Kiantone and at Patriot. In 1860, he visited the Shakers and the Oneida Community to learn about their beliefs and community structures. His vision for the future, however, was still tied to his past. Spear wrote a note to Sheldon on September 3, 1860, saying that he and Mrs. Hinckley visited Niagara Falls, "to get out of the national papers".[138] By national papers, Spear probably meant Spiritualist publications. However, as seen in the Boston trial of 1862, his reputation problems did not just melt away.

Once he joined the Abolitionist Movement, and even more so after he became a Spiritualist, John Murray Spear saw himself on the grand American stage where he might effect sweeping social change. He was consistent, if nothing else, in believing that through his work and ministry, he would make the nation and the world a better place. Spear saw himself as a dynamic leader empowered by the ethereal spirits he believed were directing both his life and his ministry. Even when he appeared to be thwarted by an event such as the 1862 trial, Spear, to use a contemporary term, just *re-invented* himself and moved on to the next stage of his work. Some would call him a charlatan, but others would simply describe him as dependably creative.

Financial scheming continued to be a component of Spear's ministry. In another letter written to Sheldon on September 1, 1860, Spear wrote about a sprit message received from Benjamin Franklin suggesting that a second volume of *The Educator* be sold for $1.00 per copy.[139] As was often the case, the message was in keeping with Franklin's own entrepreneurial writing and publishing projects, thus, giving the spirit message assured credibility.

Although Spear always considered himself to be a missionary medium, in 1861 and 1862, there emerged a subtle shift in Spear's concerns *from visionary community builder to Spiritualist businessman.* The *Sheldon Papers* demonstrate ample evidence during these years that Spear, Sheldon, and others in the newly established Sacred Order of Unionists focused on conducting business in an honest and moral fashion. For example, one proposed business venture was the purchase of the *Pilot Knob Iron Company* in Missouri. After considering the venture, Spear and Sheldon decided not to acquire the company because they were concerned that its workers might include slaves. Ironically, they also hoped that messages from the spirit world would give them special insights into certain business dealings so that they might be successful. Evidently, they saw no problem with the *insider information* these spirit messages would give them, compared to business persons who did not have such insight.

Most of the reference works and articles written about John Murray Spear make some reference to the Harmonia community's coming to an end. A few mention the demise of the Patriot colony. These resources continue, saying that Spear went to Europe during the Civil War to sell sewing machines and continue his mediumistic work. This is true. But the rest of the story of what he did there is quite interesting and all too often overlooked.

In April 1862, Thaddeus Sheldon and John Orvis formed *The Union Family Sewing Machine Company.* Spear was give a promotional role in this venture. However, the partnership was short lived. Orvis left the sewing machine company on June 3, 1862, although he was not entirely out of the picture.

On February 2, 1863, John Orvis issued a *Proclamation of the Dissolution of the Order of Sacred Unionists.*[140] In the same document, he announced that anyone who belonged to the former Order of Sacred Unionists was invited to join the new organization, the *Association for Unitive* [sic, Orvis' spelling] *and Business Purposes.*

Orvis' announcement was interesting since the Order of Sacred Unionists was supposed to last seven years which would make its last year something like the Old Testament jubilee celebration, and then be disbanded. However, this new organizational structure replaced it after only about three years. Reading between the lines, it might indicate that Orvis had grown tired of Spear's exhausting funds. Maybe Orvis thought this new structure would bring the group's finances under control. But those hunches are only speculation.

Nevertheless, there was a subtle, but obvious, difference between these two organizational structures. Spear and his colleagues moved from being a group of Spiritualists, who also had business concerns, to a group of businessmen who happened to be Spiritualists. Attention during the ensuing weeks turned to getting financial matters in proper order. An inventory was made of the location and worth of any lands owned by the Sacred Order of Unionists. This led to a reorganization of the previous group's debts. Reading between the lines, it again seems that Orvis recognized that Spear and Sheldon had gone through a considerable amount of money and obtained properties that were less than profitable. It is likely that Orvis believed he could bring a more business-like, even profitable, environment to their shared vision and work.[141] Still, the group certainly was not abandoning Spiritualism. Rather, there remained throughout 1863, and the next two years, a strong intention to improve the work of business by incorporating Spiritualist understandings into the effort.

It is quite true that in 1863, Spear went to Europe to sell sewing machines, offer his services as a medium, and spread the influence of Spiritualism (Illustration 3). It was an uncertain time, when neither the North nor the South seemed able to achieve an overwhelmingly decisive victory that would end the Civil War. Throughout this time, Thaddeus Sheldon remained in the United States. However, his continued interest, and probably what little remained of his fortune, served to fuel Spear's work.

Finally, in 1865, both John Orvis and John Sterling joined Spear in Europe. Their work was intended to aid Spear in selling sewing machines and promoting Spiritualism. Things did not go well. At one point, they took to the streets of London, searching in desperation for dealers and wholesalers who would carry their sewing machines.[142] Sterling wrote a letter to Sheldon in early 1865, in which he appears to indicate some quibbling over how Spear handled money.[143] In time, Spear came to the realization that the sewing machine business was not for him and that he needed to devote his full attention to Spiritualism, particularly healing ministries.

Handily, one of Spear's last letters to Thaddeus Sheldon, written in May, 1865, states that while in Paris, he received support from a Californian, a woman named, Miss Day.[144] In his autobiography, Spear described how he and Mrs. Hinckley, upon their return to the United States, established a new ministry based in California. Although Miss Day is not mentioned as a benefactor in Spear's autobiography, other California supporters are mentioned.

Mr. J. M. Spear.

72 Albany Street Regents Park.
(London.)

(over)

Guided and assisted by beneficent Spirit-Intelligences, Mr. S. will examine and prescribe for disease of body and mind; will delineate the character of persons when present, or by letter, and indicate their future as impressions are given him; will sketch the special capacities of young persons.

At home from 12 to 3 P.M. daily, (Sundays excepted.) Fee, Half a Guinea. Special arrangements may be made for visits.

Applications to lecture, or hold conversations on Spiritualism, will be welcomed.

Illustrations 3

The phrase, "follow the money," seems to be the *modus operandi* of the entire Spear saga. Spear was, of course, by his own definition, a missionary medium, a kind of itinerant messenger for Spiritualism whose spirit guides told him where to go. This type of ministry can be funded as a *tent-making ministry*. It is named after the style used by the Christian Apostle Paul, who continued his work as a tent-maker while he traveled to spread the Christian Gospel. Spear did something quite similar when he tried to combine selling sewing machines with his Spiritualist ministry in Europe.

Another style of missionary work is funded by donations from supporters. Upon returning to the United States, Spear admittedly chose to rely on a funding base supported by generous donors. Spear believed that was what the spirits were directing him to do.

All this business of going to Europe to sell sewing machines, giving séances, healing ministries, and returning to the United States after the Civil War might appear as "ho, hum", mildly boring stuff. What caught my eye, however, were some references that any Civil War buff would quickly note, even as I did. An example of this is a letter that Spear wrote to Thaddeus Sheldon, dated February 2, 1865. In the letter, he refers to a Spiritualist friend that he made in England, a Mr. Ferguson, who Spear calls "the Prince of Confederates".[145] This one example is no exception. Spear's letters and documents from throughout the period are quite littered with various comments on both the crisis faced by the United States in the 1850s and 1860s as well as the possibilities for change created by that crisis.

Throughout most of his life and ministry, Spear saw himself, probably subconsciously, as an actor on a stage. He had come in contact with some of the finest minds and greatest leaders of his day. He firmly believed that bold people with bold visions could change society for the better. It is a curious thing, given his extensive work as a medium, that Spear was listed in the *1864 Progressive Annual,* the Spiritualist directory, not as a medium but as a "social agitator".[146] Spear's mediumistic ministry had caused an uproar, but his colleagues evidently still valued his work in the social and political arena. One can almost envision the editors of the *Progressive Annual* talking among themselves and saying, "Well, we have to put him somewhere!" Spear, always opportunistic, saw the Civil War both as a human tragedy as well as the proverbial golden opportunity to make right those things in society that were wrong.

Spear was not alone in this matter. Thaddeus Sheldon, John Orvis, and John Sterling were also listed as "social agitators" in the *1864 Progressive Annual.* As early as April 27, 1861, not quite two weeks after the fall of *Fort Sumter,* Thaddeus Sheldon wrote of a spirit message he received from Robert Ratoul (see Chapter 9) and recorded these words:

> *The American Congress is a defunct body. The President cannot manage it and the Cabinet is not a <u>unit</u> [sic, Sheldon's underlining] … Seward is not a statesman, Cameron was selected not because of qualification but because of location. Washington is a doomed city. It had better be abandoned now than kept another twelve months.*[147]

Sheldon, no doubt, envisioned something better rising out of the ashes.

Spear also communicated similar sentiments. He was particularly upset, early in the Civil War, that the North held to the rationale that the war was predicated upon preserving the Union, as opposed to eliminating the abominable institution of slavery. He believed that if the North clearly stated an eradication of slavery rationale, then some European countries would be inclined to lend both material support as well as military troops. In one particular diatribe, written on June 11, 1863, just after the *Battle of Chancellorsville* and just weeks before the *Battle of Gettysburg*, Spear described America as a whore [*sic*, Spear's word] because it refused to make slavery the primary reason for the war which was, to his thinking, totally inconsistent with the American *Founding Fathers'* beliefs. The language in this document is incendiary, to say the least, as Spear also described America as "putrid," "decaying," and "not worth saving".[148] One may, however, agree with the overall nature of his sentiment, given this time in history and the abomination of slavery.

There are several similar documents in which Spear's attitude towards the United States was decidedly vitriolic.[149] He appeared, at times, to be totally convinced that the Civil War would result in two new nations. His hope was that the North would emerge from the ashes and form a republic where all African Americans and all women would enjoy full suffrage.

Perhaps, I am just a product of the *Post-9/11 World*, but all of this sounded a bit like treason or sedition to me. *Treason*, making war against one's own country or aiding its enemies, is probably too strong a word. On the other hand, Spear's actions, especially his relationship with "the Prince of the Confederates", did have a seditious ring about. This is so, because *sedition* includes acting, writing, or speaking against one's country, especially in time of war. Spear knew that some people thought his lectures and spirit messages contained seditious pronouncements, and he notes their accusations in his autobiography.[150]

In another era, Spear's words might have been just that. But the nature of the Civil War was different. *Slavery* was the issue that brought about the conflict, but *secession* from the Union was the environment in which the Civil War was fought. The stakes were high. Going into the Civil War, a clear geopolitical structure held together the North American continent. Mexico lay to the south and its boundaries were more or less fixed by the *Mexican War.* Canada, then a territory of Great Britain, lay to the north. The United States, as they existed prior to the Civil War, held the North American continent in a geopolitical kind of stasis. Ripped apart by the South's secession, the whole picture became very unstable and potentially dangerous.

President Lincoln, more than anything else, wanted the Union pulled back together. Thus, Lincoln chose to treat the Confederates like runaway children, not like instigators of a bloody and costly internecine war. This is why Lincoln did not push the issues of treason and sedition. He knew that accusing the South's leaders of high crimes and misdemeanors would only make it more difficult to draw them back into the Federal fold. In the aftermath of the war, only one Confederate was found guilty and executed as a traitor. That man was Henry Wirz, the commandant of the *Andersonville Prison* where so many Union soldiers suffered and died.

Did John Murray Spear and others, like Thaddeus Sheldon, commit or encourage sedition? The answer is "probably". But they got away with it because no one was pursuing such matters during the Civil War. The focus was placed on reuniting the states under one flag, not on punishing the transgressors. It is important to note, also, that Spear and his colleagues were not the only Americans in the North expressing a harsh view of the United States during the Civil War. Finally, Spear and Sheldon's communications were largely private. It would have taken someone inside their

Spiritualist network to have betrayed their thoughts and writings to the government.

What, then, became of Ferguson, Spear's "Prince of the Confederates" friend? When Spear writes about this person, he is almost certainly referring to *Jesse Babcock Ferguson*, a pastor who was quite famous as an orator and preacher in the antebellum South. Born in Philadelphia, raised in Virginia, and trained as a printer, Ferguson first taught at a rural Presbyterian school before becoming an itinerant preacher in Kentucky. In 1846, he was called to preach at a *Church of Christ* congregation in Nashville, TN. This denomination was also known as the *Disciples of Christ*.

By 1852, Ferguson broke ranks with Church of Christ theology and embraced the concept of universal salvation and began to teach and preach both Unitarian and Universalist doctrines. Several attempts were made to remove him from his pulpit. However, Ferguson found great support from most of his congregation and continued to serve them until he was finally forced to resign in 1857. A son of the South, Ferguson believed in slavery, but he also believed that in the next life, slaves would be free.

After Nashville was occupied by Federal troops in February 1862, Ferguson departed for England, where he most likely came into contact with John Murray Spear. There Ferguson, as did Spear,[151] promoted the idea of an international congress that would mediate the differences between the Union and the Confederacy. Returning to Richmond, VA, he found no support for his ideas. Later, Ferguson returned to Tennessee, where Federal troops seized him, and placed him under something like house arrest for the remainder of the war.

When the Civil War ended, Ferguson went to Washington where he sought to lend aid to *President Andrew Johnson*. This was no shot-in-the-dark initiative, as Johnson had been both Ferguson's friend and a member of Ferguson's congregation back in Nashville before the Civil War. And, in what must have seemed to John Murray Spear an incredible moment and an incredible opportunity, while in Washington, Ferguson hand-delivered spirit messages from John Murray Spear to President Johnson.[152] What those messages contained we do not know. It is not known what impact they may have had on President Johnson, whose presidency was among the most inept and saddest in American history. However, Johnson's political stance was against granting full citizenship, including voting rights, to former slaves. He also supported rapid restoration of citizen rights and privileges to former Confederates. Given what we know of John Murray Spear and his spirit friends, we can guess that the messages Ferguson hand-delivered from Spear to Johnson made little or no impact.

John Murray Spear had long desired to play a role in trans-forming American society and, perhaps, even understood himself to be spirit-called to such a role. Having Ferguson deliver spirit messages to the White House and place them in the hands of the President of the United States certainly must have made Spear feel that he was finally achieving that long-awaited goal. Given the tone of Johnson's presidency, which did little for freed African Americans and simply forgave and restored the Confederacy, Spear must have subsequently felt a profound sense of failure. That was the biggest role that Spear ever played on the American stage, but it was a flop. Like the 1858 convention, Spear made no mention of it in his autobiography. Still, it is fascinating to think that the efforts of the Spiritualist leader of the little community on the banks of the Kiantone Creek, even if unsuccessful, reached all the way to the White House.

As noted above, Spear, upon his return from Europe, went to California to work as a missionary medium. There he stayed for several years, making two side trips to Utah to meet with the Mormons and learn from their teachings. Eventually, when he was about 68 years old, Spear returned to Kiantone to write his autobiography. The world had changed greatly during Spear's years of Spiritualist missionary work. His autobiography, unfortunately, offers little insight about how those changes impacted him. Perhaps, we will never fully know.

CONCLUSION

The Kiantone area has always had a mystical aura about it. In 1680, Charles II of England, stipulated to William Penn that the 42nd parallel north latitude would be the northern boundary of the Pennsylvania Colony. The Kiantone Springs emerge almost precisely on that marked latitude. In 1795, when an early settler, *James McMahan*, came up the Conewango Creek on his way north, he found Indian cornfields and longhouses where the Kiantone Creek enters the Conewango Creek. The people living there were Cornplanter's people.

A few years before, in 1787, two surveyors, Andrew Ellicott and Andrew Proctor, completed charting the northern boundary of Pennsylvania.[153] Andrew Ellicott was a surveyor of note. He surveyed the boundaries of Washington, D.C. for the new American government and also, eventually, was named as the country's *Surveyor General*. His brother, *Joseph*, was a surveyor for the *Holland Land Company* and the Town of Ellicott was named for him. Andrew Proctor's biographical background, unfortunately, is obscure.

From August 25 to September 9, 1787, the survey was stopped because of conflicts with local Native Americans. Their leader,

Cornplanter, reportedly did not object to the survey work, but young Seneca men in his town did object. They wanted what they termed a *treaty*, i.e., alcohol. The surveyors provided the liquid spirits, they all feasted together, and the survey work continued.

By 1885, the milestones marking the New York and Pennsylvania boundary had, in many cases, been damaged or removed. This necessitated repeating the survey work that was done in 1787, including the section where the surveyors had encountered Cornplanter and the young Seneca men. The *Report of the Regents' Boundary Commission upon the New York and Pennsylvania Boundary* was presented on April 22, 1886. It included the discovery that the boundary markers stones were off, in some places, by as much as 1,000 feet. The commission designated the place where the measurements were most inaccurate as an "enormous error".[154] They offered the explanation that this extreme error was probably caused by the rough and irregular topography and some unusual anomaly that threw off the original surveyors' magnetic measurement results by one degree. Rather than forcing Pennsylvanians to become New Yorkers, or *vice versa*, the boundary was left where it was.

The *Boundary Commission* report indicated that the greatest boundary errors were near Kiantone, New York.

AFTERWORD

From Ulysses S. Grant to Lucy

There remain some unresolved questions and hunches about the Kiantone saga that others might wish to pursue. It has been fun writing this book, but I have deliberately left some enjoyment for others who may wish to engage in some historical sleuth work. My only hope is that you will have as much fun as I did! My only request is that if you discover more about Kiantone, please share that information with the Fenton History Center-Museum and Library, the Warren County Historical Museum, and the Darlington Memorial Collection, University of Pittsburgh.

Of particular note are the *Sheldon Papers*. Obviously, Thaddeus Sheldon himself realized the historical value of these documents, records, and letters. About 73 years after his death they were discovered in a small metal box. In the box was a note stipulating that the documents were to be preserved, perhaps in one of the planned Harmonia temple cornerstones. The note was significant, because it indicated that even at the time of his death, Sheldon still held hope that Harmonia' grand city might yet be built at some time in the future.

After Sheldon's death, the documents somehow wound up in an attic, probably in his home. There they lay for decades in the box until Mrs. Margaret M. Fish, Sheldon's granddaughter, discovered them in 1940. Mrs. Fish stated in a letter to Ernest C. Miller dated April 17, 1957, that the attic was in her home;[155] but this does not resolve the location issue, since some of her correspondence comes from Syracuse, NY. Her August 13, 1951, letter to Mr. Miller shows her Syracuse address scratched out on her stationary and her new Randolph address added. My hunch, however, is that the trunk was found in Randolph in a home that once belonged to Sheldon, but eventually came to his granddaughter. If someone wanted to pursue this issue, it would take some digging into records and deeds.

Mrs. Fish's identity is interesting. According to some accounts, she was Sheldon's granddaughter, while others refer to her as his niece. Mrs. Fish's letter to Ernest Miller dated April 17, 1957, appears to put the matter at rest, since she refers to Sheldon as "my Grandfather".

Mrs. Fish recognized the historical worth of the *Sheldon Papers*, but there is no clear indication that she was well versed in Sheldon's activities nor those of his Spiritualist friends. For example, in an August 13, 1951, type-written letter, Mrs. Fish added a hand-written question, "Do the enclosed Deed and Mortgage [*sic*, Mrs. Fish's capitalizations] have anything to do with the proposed colony at Patriot, Ind [*sic*, her abbreviation for Indiana]?" Although she may not have been aware of the details, we are eternally grateful for her insight and her understanding that the papers needed to be seen by historians.

Mrs. Fish first shared them with *William S. Bailey* (1869-1953), a life-long Jamestown resident who was phenomenally involved as a civic leader and prominent businessman. His life, in fact, would be a worthy subject for another local history book, or, at least, a substantial pamphlet. During his long life, he served Chautauqua Institution as a newspaper editor, first for the *Chautauqua Assembly Herald*, and then its successor publication, the *Chautauqua Daily*.

With two partners, Bailey also founded the *Chautauqua School of Nursing*. This unique institution was set up as a correspondence course that taught nursing practices to students in every state and several foreign countries. The school operated successfully for 35 years before merging with the *Chicago School of Nursing*.

As a young child, Mr. Bailey was taken to Chautauqua Institution, founded in 1874, where he remembered being introduced to *President Ulysses S. Grant*. He died in 1953, at age 84, having lived a long life that stretched from just after the Civil War to the dawn of television. The year he died, another famous Jamestown native, *Lucille Ball*, began her successful and ground-breaking television comedy series. Thus, Mr. Bailey's extraordinary life stretched from Ulysses S. Grant to Lucy. Remarkable!

An avid amateur local historian, Mr. Bailey spent considerable time during the 1930s, researching the Harmonia saga. He gave local lectures on the subject, most notably a speech presented to Jamestown's *University Club* on site at Kiantone on June 27, 1924. He also wrote several articles for various Jamestown newspapers. The frustrating thing about Mr. Bailey's Kiantone articles is that he seldom named his sources and footnoted nothing. Nevertheless, he obviously gained a great deal of knowledge about the Kiantone experiment and did blaze a trail for historians who came after him.

Mr. Bailey's confidence in his knowledge about Kiantone could, at times, be somewhat amusing. In a November 18, 1933, *Jamestown Evening Journal* article he wrote, "Altho [sic, Bailey's spelling] the history of the strange settlement 75 years ago at Spiritual Springs in the Kiantone valley is now practically complete . . ." In the article, Bailey went on to describe a partial exploration of the tunnel. This was seven years before the *Sheldon Papers* came to light, and it may well be that Mr. Bailey had, by 1933, exhausted almost all the available documentation.

After Mrs. Fish's discovery of the *Sheldon Papers*, Mr. Bailey wrote an article entitled, "Wealth of Lore Dealing with Spiritualist Community at Kiantone Found in Attic", published in the *Jamestown Post*, November 26, 1940. At the time of writing that article, he had possession of the *Sheldon Papers*, but had not yet begun to study them in depth. He was 71 years old, and perhaps he was just running out of steam for major research projects. In any event, Mrs. Fish wrote a letter to Ernest Miller on April 17, 1957, noting that she had given Bailey some of Sheldon's letters and papers. She told Miller in the same letter that she had subsequently received correspondence from Bailey saying he thought the materials should be placed in the "Jamestown Library", but she did not know if he did that before his death. There is no clear paper trail showing how Bailey used the *Sheldon Papers*, other than the aforementioned newspaper article.

In 1947, Mrs. Fish lent her copy of *The Educator*, and Thaddeus Sheldon's journal to Ernest Miller of Warren, PA. Mr. Miler was the President of the *West Penn Oil Company, Inc.* and a dedicated amateur local historian. He was, at that time, in the process of amassing an enormous amount of information about John Murray Spear and Harmonia. Miller's plan was to publish a "complete history" [*sic*, his term] of the Kiantone saga in 1953, to mark the centennial of Harmonia's beginning. As far as I know, he never completed that work.

Letters written in 1951 and 1957, indicate Mrs. Fish's occasional and understandable concern that Mr. Miller had not yet returned the book and journal to her. Reading his responses to her inquiries, one almost gets the impression that Mr. Miller felt a type of protective need to retain possession of the resources, even though they rightfully belonged to Mrs. Fish. At one point, he actually invited her to come to Warren and visit the materials and view the other resources he had collected.

It appears from Mr. Miller's letter, dated April 1957, that he had returned the journal and book to Mrs. Fish. But his research on Kiantone was extensive. Mr. Miller noted in a letter written to T.D. Seymour Bassett on December 16, 1947, and housed with the *Sheldon Collection*, that he visited the Harmonia site in 1941. He further stated that the only lingering signs of the colony were remnants of the hotel (actually located in Pennsylvania), some circles of rocks upon which the octagon cottages had been erected, and the entrance to the tunnel. He also noted that he collected so many resources about Kiantone that he had to move those materials into an office at the *Woolworth* store building in Warren, PA. Having experienced my own home being overrun with these materials, I had to laugh when I read his words!

A word should be noted about the location of the University of Pittsburgh's Darlington Memorial Collection, where the *Sheldon Papers* have been housed since Ernest Miller placed them there on February 22, 1960, presumably with the permission of Mrs. Fish or upon her death. The collection is housed in the University of Pittsburgh's *Cathedral of Learning*. It is a rather astonishing structure that was begun in 1926, when the nation was in the midst of a financial boom. Before the work was completed, *The Great Depression* hit and the project was brought to a halt. To complete the work, everyone in the city was invited to make a financial gift to the project, ranging from children's pennies to large corporate gifts. Subsequently, the building was completed in 1937, much to the credit of the city and its supportive residents and businesses.

Soaring 42 stories high, the Cathedral of Learning consists of a student center built in the style of a Gothic cathedral with, remarkably, a skyscraper emerging from its roof where one would normally expect to see a steeple. Within the building are libraries, classrooms, and offices. The Darlington Memorial Collection is located on the 6th floor of this unique structure. The Cathedral of Learning is astonishing, indeed, and hauntingly reminiscent of the lavish structures once envisioned for Harmonia.

One of the things that I always thought I would find in my research and, yet, never did, was a comparison of the proposed Domain's grand architectural community in the Kiantone Valley to Jordan's ancient city, *Petra*. Established around the Sixth Century B.C., and located in present-day Jordan, Petra (translated, "rock") was home to a large nomadic Nabataean Arab commercial center dealing primarily in spices. The Romans took it over around 1000 B.C. In the 12th Century A.D., the Crusaders built a large fort at Petra, but later abandoned it. After that it was known to local people, but essentially became one of the *lost wonders of the ancient world.* In 1812, Bedouins showed it to Swiss explorer, *Johann Ludwig Burckhardt.*

Petra is located in a deep desert rift valley surrounded by hills, about five hours south, by bus, of present day Amman. Its overall size is somewhat comparable to the Kiantone Valley and surrounding hillsides. In Petra there are temples, tombs, and a treasury, all with an elegant façade dug into the rust-colored sandstone canyon walls. There is also a marketplace colonnade. Petra has frequently been used as a movie location, most notably and recently in *Indiana Jones and the Temple of Doom.* Having visited Petra myself, I shouted out loud in the movie theater when I saw the Jones character riding into the hidden desert city. (By now you have probably decided never to go to libraries or the movies with me for fear of embarrassment.)

Petra was one of the distinguished "discoveries" of the early 19th Century. This "new" archeological site was well-documented. One would think that learned men of that general time period, such as John Murray Spear and Horace Greeley, would have made the connection to the general geography of the Kiantone Valley and Harmonia's planned city, but apparently, no one did. Probably, given that most of the Domain's proposed buildings were never constructed, it was simply too much of a leap for other historians to connect the dots. However, I do think the comparison would make a worthy topic for a term paper. Perhaps some high school or college student will make good use of it someday.

The property where the tunnel is located, as descrobed previously, changed hands after the demise of the Spiritualist experiment. Currently, as noted in Chapter 5, it belongs to John Kost, who inherited it from his father. The elder Mr. Kost purchased the land, which contained a more recently built summer cottage, from Gerald Staples. In the *Sheldon Papers,* there is a document detailing an unpublished interview with Mr. Staples, probably conducted by Ernest Miller on January 13, 1949. The text follows:

Mr. Staples was formerly a contractor and has had a cottage at Spiritual Springs for years. His deed is from Emry A. Studevant and Lynn K. Sturdevant dated October 17, 1914 . . . The mineral spring is on the very corner of Staples' land and right on the New York-Pennsylvania State line . . . Mr. Staples, while still a contractor, commensing [sic] digging out the old tunnel the Spiritualists had started . . . One of his workers narrowly missed being trapped in the tunnel due to falling earth so the work was abandoned . . .

. . . Strange happenings have taken place several times while Staples and party have been at his cabin but Staples was careful to explain

that he is not a spiritualist [sic] though he cannot explain what he actually saw. For example, once at night they ran out of firewood and one of the men volunteered to go to the next farm and get some; after he had been gone only a few minutes the rest of the party heard a loud series of noises like boards being pulled off of a house. They got a lantern and walked down toward the last oval house and yelled for their friend, being sure that he was ripping the boards off to use as firewood. It developed he was in another direction and rather far away. He finally heard the party and joined them and reported he had heard the same noises but thought they were tearing the planks off the house themselves. An examination of the oval house made at once revealed no planks missing and no cause for the noise.

In the same interview, Staples revealed that the last house, as noted in other sources, fell down ten years prior to his purchasing the property in 1907. How the timbers might have been ripped off at least ten years later leads one to suspect a story concocted around a campfire. Mr. Staples, at the time of his death, was a highly respected citizen and recently retired City Court clerk. Still, I wonder if he did not also possess a wonderful sense of humor. (BOO!)

The tunnel was excavated during the time that Staples owned the land. This was chronicled by William S. Bailey in his 1933 *Jamestown Evening Journal* article. The digging was no easy task, complicated by both accumulated silt and flooding from the springs. Staples used a power pump and, eventually, was able to dig fifty feet slanting downward and into the side of the hill where the tunnel was located. He found a well-constructed tunnel, lined with wood, much like a coal tunnel. Contrary to what Mark Cheney reported in 1924, the tunnel was only about four and a half feet tall and three feet wide. It gradually wound down, via a series of turns, to a depth about 12 feet below the surface. A few artifacts were found, including a glass whale oil lamp. Mr. Staples realized, quite rightly, that the tunnel, as it existed in 1933, was a dangerous place. Concluding his exploration, he covered it with a concrete enclosure. Again, the danger cannot be overstated and today it is well known that Mr. Kost's property is clearly marked with *No Trespassing* signs.

Spear's booklet, *Twenty Years on the Wing: Narrative of Travels and Labors as a Missionary Sent Forth by the Association of Beneficents in the Spirit-Land*, is one of the primary keys to this book. Norman P. Carlson, a volunteer at the Fenton History Center-Museum and Library in Jamestown, gave me a photocopy of this resource that he had obtained from the *State University of New York at Fredonia's Daniel A. Reed Library (General Archives Collection)*. Later, I learned that SUNY at Fredonia's copy of the pamphlet was photocopied from an original in the *United States Library of Congress*.

I was thrilled to gain access to this resource, as the only other copies I could locate via inter-library loan were in the *Library of Congress* and a public library in Wisconsin. After Norman graciously shared his copy with me, it was several hours before I noted that the title page bore the signature, "Houdini". I knew that Harry Houdini, the famous magician, had at one time practiced Spiritualism and visited *Lilly Dale*, founded in 1879, the oldest continuing Spiritualist community in America and located near the northern Chautauqua County village of Cassadaga. (Forget the question about why Western New York has proffered so many religious experiments! Why is it that Chautauqua County is such a hotbed for faith-based activities?)

Houdini is particularly interesting. At one point, he took a great interest in Spiritualism, but later turned against it. His negative response went as far as to lobby the United States Congress to enact legislation prohibiting it, similar to what Germany has done in our own time regarding *Scientology*. Anyway, I spent the next several months thinking that Houdini had given his signed copy of Spear's pamphlet to SUNY at Fredonia. Only after eventually talking with the library's curator did I learn that all SUNY at Fredonia had was a photocopy of the original pamphlet, with Houdini's signature, from the Library of Congress. Still, I was very grateful to obtain a photocopy of this primary resource.

From the verdant hills and lush valleys of Kiantone and its rural environs, including the Town of Carroll and the village of Frewsburg, sprang forth one of our nation's most esteemed Supreme Court justices, *Robert Houghwout Jackson*. (Yes, Harry Potter fans, that's "Houghwout", not "Hogwart".) Jackson was born in 1902, at Spring Creek, PA, about 25 miles southwest of Kiantone; but he and his family moved to Frewsburg, NY, near his grandparents' home in the Kiantone area, when he was ten years old. A bright lad, Jackson attended neither college nor law school, but served as a legal apprentice and became a member of the *New York Bar* when he was only 21. He became a great courtroom and business lawyer, respected citizen, and active Democrat Party worker.

While serving one year of his law apprenticeship in Albany, New York State's capital, Jackson caught the eye of *Franklin Delano Roosevelt*. When FDR was elected governor and subsequently president, he brought Jackson along and appointed him to various legal positions. In 1940, FDR appointed Jackson to the position of *Attorney General* and in 1941, FDR placed him on the *Supreme Court*. After WWII, President Truman sent Jackson to Europe where, in Nuremburg, Germany, he served as *chief prosecutor of the Nuremburg trials of Nazi war criminals*. When he died suddenly in 1954, the United States lost its top justice (though Jackson was never the Chief Justice) and one of its greatest lawyers.[156]

What is particularly remarkable about Justice Robert Jackson is that he was well aware of Harmonia's history at Kiantone. Most likely, he heard tales about it from his grandfather. One interesting account, dated in 1924, is about *L. J. Bennett*, a former pastor of the *Lander Methodist Church*, located just across the border in Pennsylvania. Pastor Bennett recalled that when he served that church in 1879 and 1880, *Robert Jackson*, grandfather of Robert H. Jackson, came to Lander and asked the pastor to preach at the Fairbanks schoolhouse near the hamlet of Kiantone. Mr. Jackson said things were going on there that simply were not right. He described these happenings to Pastor Bennett, but the pastor thought it best not to repeat them in his recollection. A good hunch is that those unmentionable things had to do with some resurgence of Spiritualist activities or Free Love, or both.

A review of Jackson's legal statements indicates a dedication to the American commitment to freedom of religion. Consider the following:

The very purpose of the Bill of Rights was to withdraw certain subjects from the vicissitudes of political controversy, to place them beyond the reach of majorities and officials to establish them as legal principles to be applied by the courts. One's right to life, liberty, and property, to free speech, a free press, freedom of worship and assembly, and other fundamental rights, may not be submitted to vote; they depend on the outcome of no elections.

West Virginia Board of Education
vs. Barnette, 319, U.S. 624 (1943) at 638.

The wrong of these things, as I see it, is not in the money the victims part with half so much as in the mental and spiritual poison they get. But that is precisely the thing the Constitution put beyond the reach of the prosecutor, for the price of freedom of religion [sic, italics added] or of speech or of the press is that we must put up with, or even pay for, a good deal of rubbish ... I would dismiss the indictment and have done with this business of judicially examining other people's faiths.

United States v. Ballard,
322, U.S. 78 (1944) at 95

It is interesting, I think, to compare Jackson's statements above to a letter he wrote to Miss Ruth Sternberg, a Frewsburg resident, on July 7, 1951, indicating his opinion of the Harmonia community. In this letter Jackson mentions that he had sent Miss Sternberg a copy of William Bailey's 1924 speech delivered to the University Club. It is intriguing, I think, to consider that this great justice had a copy of Bailey's speech readily available in his files. Jackson also mentions several histories about Spiritualism, including references to John Murray Spear, available in the *Congressional Library*. Finally, he refers to Spiritualism as, using his words, "a cult".[157]

There is a tendency in modern society to use the word *cult* to refer to any faith system designated as unorthodox. Rather than just a simple observation, often this designation is assigned in a punitive or ridiculing manner. It is, therefore, interesting to note that while Robert H. Jackson wrote Supreme Court summary judgments that extolled the American right to religion, like many of us, in his private thoughts he believed differently. Reading his letter to Miss Stern, we see that Jackson, as we tend to do, created a system of who is orthodox and who is not orthodox compared to, at least, Spiritualists in general and John Murray Spear in particular. Again, this is another topic that could be further explored in an academic paper. My reason for lifting Jackson's letter here is simply to raise, once again, the hope I first stated in the *Introduc-*

tion, namely that we might all be advocates for religious freedom, especially in the midst of the troubling times in which we live. However, I cannot, and my hope is that neither can you, condone any religious system that attacks the life and liberty of others.

In 1950, the *Sheldon Papers* drew the interest of *Arthur E. Bestor, Jr.*, an associate professor of history at the *University of Illinois*. Mr. Bestor, born in Chautauqua County in 1908, was the son of one of Chautauqua Institution's finest presidents. He took an interest in Harmonia while doing research about the various communitarian communities that sprang up across rural America in the mid-19th Century, particularly those with ties to Charles Fourier and Robert Owen. Mr. Bestor's work resulted in his book, *Backwood Utopias: The Sectarian and Owenite Phases of Communitarian Socialism in America, 1663-1829*. The book is out-of-print, but I found a copy of it on the Internet. Alas, it contains only a solitary and brief mention of Kiantone's Harmonia, a listing in a table entitled "Other English Language Communities" on page 283. What makes the entry significant, however, is that Bestor quite rightly cites Harmonia as not being directly related to either Owen or Fournier. This is correct, since neither Spear nor his colleagues were directly related to either of these communitarian leaders. It should be noted, however, that Spear did know about Owen and he appreciated Owen's endeavors.

In 1958, Edward M. Byrne, a reporter for *The Jamestown (N.Y) Sun*, wrote a lengthy article, "Harmonia, Town that Love Built, Killed by Hate, Fear, Suspicion." This article contains the newspaperman's observation: "An accurate portrayal of it would be impossible, because of the terror, fear, and hate which the local residents felt toward these people." Other than the episode when local people destroyed the "living" machine, there did not appear to be much overt negative response to the Spiritualists at Kiantone. Byrne's title for the article seems rather like overkill, compared to the eyewitness accounts of Harmonia provided by Oliver F. Chase, Mark Cheney, and Arthur Northrop. While those eye witnesses cast doubtful eyes toward what transpired at Harmonia, they do not appear to be laced with hateful venom. Could it be that, in 1958, the recent McCarthy hearings in Congress had some effect on Mr. Byrne's telling of the Harmonia story?

Periodically during the 1900s, various articles about Harmonia appeared in the Jamestown and other newspapers and in various tourist and local interest publications. Some of these were quite good, while others contained significant historical errors. But, this is not a simple tale, as noted in the *Note about Resources.* I note the errors, not to denigrate any previous researches and writers who tackled this subject, but simply as a *mea culpa* to others who may - although I hope different - one day find an occasional error in my own work.

This brings to an end my telling of Kiantone's saga. I have thoroughly enjoyed reopening the window into this fascinating and fun aspect of Chautauqua County's history. My sincere hope is that others will further delve into the story and, then, re-tell it from their own perspective and with their own insights.

ACKNOWLEDGEMENTS

This book was one of those projects that endeared old friends to my heart and introduced me to new friends and colleagues. Quite literally, I could not have completed the task without them.

I am indebted to *Beth Moses*, who served as primary editor for the book. Her spiritual insights and strong desire for literary clarity significantly aided in shaping the book's content.

Sandy Ahlgren and *Janet Jacobs*, both excellent spellers and grammarticians, also spent hours pouring over the manuscript as it was completed, chapter by chapter.

Duane Priset and *Bob Whitaker*, both clergy, provided excellent theological and church history critiques. I am always amazed by how knowledgeable these two men are, coupled with their great humility. Dr. Priset was very generous in giving me his article about the Wesley family ghost.

A host of research librarians assisted me. Some are unnamed, but all donated their valuable expertise and time. Most notable is *Marcia Grodsky* , curator, of the Darlington Memorial Collection at the University of Pittsburgh. She patiently helped me find my way through the extensive *Sheldon Papers* and responded cheerfully to numerous e-mails and phone calls. *Silva M. Blake* and *John Magill*, of The Williams Research Center, The Historic New Orleans Collection, led both Ron Jacobs and me through the center's 19th Century shipyard records. I was relieved several months after Hurricane Katrina to learn that the collection had survived the storm, but remain deeply concerned for all whose lives were impacted by that terrible event. *John Farrance*, Research Librarian, and *Linda Benedict*, Archive Librarian, at Hobart and William Smith Colleges, Geneva, NY, aided me in a research detour as I explored the Spiritualist beliefs of *William Smith*, founder of the women's college. At one time I thought William Smith might have been a benefactor of John Murray Spear's ministry, since Spear mentions a man by that name in his autobiography. However, I abandoned that notion when I discovered the two men did not travel in similar Spiritualist circles, nor did major events in their lives happen at the same time.

Extraordinary thanks are also extended to the *Oil City Council on the Arts* for generously allowing me to use the photo of their Cornplanter statue on the cover of this book.

Carol Drake, at the Robert H. Jackson Center in Jamestown was very helpful. I am delighted to see this wonderful new addition to Jamestown's culture and history.

Kara Jensen, a Purdue University student, spent hours deciphering many of the *Sheldon Papers* that my eyesight simply would not allow me to read. She is a very bright and creative woman and loves a good mystery, so she was an excellent choice for this work.

Christie Herbst, editor of the *Jamestown Post-Journal*, gathered up materials about William S. Bailey and sent them to me. She is obviously a busy woman, but took time to supply me with the information I needed.

A host of persons dedicated to local history provided excellent guidance and support. These included *Barry Brown, Janet Hendricks,* and *Erlene Leap* in Indiana's Switzerland County, *Barbara Huffman* and *Charles Parrish*, both Ohio River historians, and Janet Scott of Conneautville, PA, who steered me towards studying

Cornplanter in greater depth. Norman P. Carlson, a volunteer at the Fenton History Center-Museum and Library, was a virtual cornucopia of helpful information and resources. *Michelle Gray,* manager, and *James Davis,* summer intern, at the Warren County Historical Society were extremely helpful. The good folks at the Chautauqua County Historical Society McClurg Museum also shared their files and records with me.

Four professional historians also proved quite helpful. *Karen Livsey,* a genealogist whose work includes activities at the Fenton History Center-Museum and Library, and *Mel Feather,* a retired Frewsburg Central School history teacher, each did a careful read of the manuscript and offered insightful corrections and suggestions. Mel put me in contact with Mr. Kost so that I could visit the tunnel site. Many thanks to Mary Jane Blustein, a retired history teacher and founding member of the Monroe County Civil War Roundtable, who helped me see the role Cuba played in the years leading up to the Civil War. *Susan Hill,* an ordained Spiritualist clergywoman, gave me the kind of insights that could only come from an active Spiritualist. I am indebted to both her and the Chesterfield Spiritualist Camp in Chesterfield, IN, for their warm hospitality, wonderful educational program, and Spiritualist art exhibits. Having chuckled often during this project, I was relieved to hear Susan say that Spiritualists are often both fun and funny. There is a self-effacing charm about that aspect of Spiritualism that other faiths would do well to adopt. As I remind myself each time I look in a mirror, God has a wonderful sense of humor!

Many thanks, also, to *P. T. Wilson,* a United Methodist clergyman, for discussing this book project with me and for introducing me to Susan Hill.

Jessie Hoag, a student teacher, steered me to map making tools on the Internet. I have a hunch that she will make a great teacher!

Ron Jacobs, Janet's husband, threw himself into researching the river voyage chapter. His work was a big help in bringing more clarity to what I found to be a profoundly fascinating aspect of the Harmonia story.

My friends and colleagues at the *Monroe County Civil War Roundtable*, including *Steve Rolfe* and *Mark Acres*, listened to me babble on about the book for over a year. Being in touch with them helped me realize that I am not the only 21st Century person living in the 19th Century!

There was a group of faithful friends who also listened for hours to my monologues about Kiantone and its history. *Colleen Anderson*, as well as *Jon and Karen Putnam*, provided gracious hospitality when I was on site in Jamestown doing research. *Bessie Adams* and *Janet Jacobs*, Ron's wife, drove me to Western New York to do research when I could not drive myself. They provided a captive audience in the car as I told them about the book. *Vern Ahlgren*, Sandy's husband, lent heartfelt support to the project. *Joyce and Walt Dahlgren* listened as I talked for hours about Kiantone, and then lent me a great book about quilts used as signs along the Underground Railroad. *Bryn Ramsey* and *Brenda Whitaker* patiently listened to me talking *ad nauseaum* about the book, and *Debbie Delaney*, more than once, pulled me back to earth with her Biblical insights. Debbie's husband, Mark Delaney, lent a hand with computer tasks at a time when both he and Debbie were busy with their new infant daughter, Addison. *David V. W.* and *June Owen* were incredibly supportive throughout the project. David kept me digging for Ohio River details and June made the trip to Vevay and Patriot, IN possible.

Dan Heise, Author Services Representative, at AuthorHouse, Inc., helped shepherd the book from its inception to its completion. His comments and suggestions were always helpful. I am most grateful for his deep patience.

If I have left out anyone, I can only hope they will forgive me. This has been a big project and I had help from many friends along the way and made many new friends, too. I am very thankful for everyone who lent assistance.

Finally, I am grateful to my mother, the late *Alice M. Cronin*. She led me back to Kiantone for rest and recreation when she was old. In doing so, she also pointed me toward a new project that kept me happily occupied for many, many days. It was her final earthly blessing to me.

APPENDIX I

ORDER OF SACRED UNIONISTS

Author's Note: The following material is from John Murray Spear's autobiographical pamphlet, pp. 28-30. It is provided exactly as it appears in the pamphlet. The reader may wish to particularly note the "precepts of this order", which number twelve and are stated in King James English and mandatory ("shalt") language. Thus they have a "Neo-Ten Commandment" character.

January 1, 1861, an organization was founded under spirit direction, called "The Sacred Order of Unionists," which was to terminate its business contracts at the end of seven years. Its general purposes are expressed substantially thus: To unite man to man, nation to nation, planet to planet. To abolish war in all its forms, and to promote universal peace. To organize various beneficent and co-operative institutions, which, without injuring the rich, would greatly aid to help educate the poor and improvident classes. To establish such religious institutions and ceremonies as are in harmony with man's nature, and tend to his highest culture. To establish a series of measures which will encourage industry, render labor honorable, remunerative, and attractive. To institute means by which education may be made thorough, equal, and universal. To secure to all a right for the cultivation of soil for useful purposes. To advise and encourage all the important sciences and the visual arts. To teach of the intimate and sacred relation which exists between the material and spiritual worlds. To aid and encourage inventions in the use of their powers for human achievement. To open new fields of thought, institute new and unitary methods of labor and of daily life, and encourage perpetual progress, and so instruct mankind that they may bring heaven down to earth and lift earth up to heaven.

The following were the precepts of this order: --

I.   Thou shalt be strictly just in all thy deals and in thy intercourse with thy fellow-men.

II.   If thou shall seest thy neighbor at fault in word or deed, thou shalt teach him in the way of everlasting life, and lead him therein.

III.   Thou shalt not cover the goods of another, in thought, word, or deed.

IV.   Thou shalt make it thy daily prayer to so walk before thy fellow-man that thy example may be worth of universal imitation.

V.   To the extent of the individual and social power thou shalt contribute to the virtue, society, industry, neatness, order, and happiness of thy kind.

VI.   It shall be thy pleasure to aid the sick, the distress, the poor, and the oppressed; to weep with those that weep, and rejoice with those that rejoice.

VII.   Thou shalt not commit adultery of any name or nature in thy thought, by thy heart, thy eye, or overt act.

VIII.   Thou shalt welcome all new thoughts, retain the good and eschew the evil.

IX.   Thou shalt avoid all harsh, unseemly, or angry debate, and thy affirmation shall be yea, and thy denial nay.

X.   Thou shall strive to so perfect thy dress that the whole body and spirit shall be enlarged and improved thereby.

XI.   Thou shalt eat of such food as shall be conducive to the highest health and harmony, and shall best fit thee for thy daily labors.

XII.   Thou shalt ever speak the truth, whatever may be the cost to thee or others , reserving to thyself the right to decide when and where thou wilt speak, and when to be silent.

BIBLIOGRAPHY

Note: this Bibliography consists of those primary, secondary, and tertiary resources used in researching this book. There are two additional extensive bibliographies prepared by Gregory Yaw and Russell Duino. Copies of both may be found at the Fenton History Center-Museum and Library, the Warren Historical Society, and the Darlington Memorial Collection in the University of Pittsburgh's library. In addition, I used the documents found at the Switzerland Public Library in Vevay, IN, located in the "Mount Alpheus" file, but they have not been arranged into a calendar or card file at this time.

BOOKS, PAMPHLETS, AND ARTICLES IN BOOKS

Bestor, Arthur Eugene, Junior. *Backwoods Utopias, The Sectarian Origins and Owenite Phase of Communitarian Socialism in the United States,* University of Pennsylvania Press, Second Edition, Philadelphia, 1970.

Chase, Oliver F. "The Kiantone Movement", *Centennial History of Chautauqua County II,* Chautauqua History Co., Jamestown, NY, 1904.

Clark, Maj. E. W. *Report of the Regents' Boundary Commission Upon The New York and Pennsylvania Boundary,* Weed, Parsons, and Company, Legislative Printers, Albany, 1886.

Crocker, Kathleen and Currie, Jane. *Images of America: Chautauqua Lake Region*, Arcadia Publishing, Charleston, SC, 2002.

Crocker, Kathleen and Currie, Jane. *Images of America: Jamestown*, Arcadia Publishing, Charleston, SC, 2004.

Cronin, Deborah K. *Holy Ground: Celtic Christian Spirituality*, Upper Room Books, Nashville, TN, 1999.

Cross, Whitney R. *The Burned Over District: The Social and Intellectual History of Enthusiastic Religion in Western New York, 1800-1850*, Cornell University Press, Ithaca, NY, 1950.

Downs, John P., editor-in-charge. "Chapter XXI", *History of Chautauqua County, New York, and Its People, Vol. I.*, American Historical Society, Inc., Boston, 1921.

Duino, Russell. "Utopian Theme with Variations: John Murray Spear and His Kiantone Domain", *Pennsylvania History, Vol. XXIX, Number 2*, April 1962.

Edson, Obed. *History of Chautauqua County, N.Y.*, W. A. Fergusson and Company, Boston, 1894.

Garvey, Joan B. and Mary Lou Widmer. *Beautiful Crescent: A History of New Orleans*, Garner Press, Inc., New Orleans, LA, 1982.

Hardinge, Emma. *Modern American Spiritualism: A Twenty Years' Record of the Communion Between Earth and the World of Spirits*, University Books, Hyde Park, NY, 1870. (First Edition published, 1870.)

Hoover, William N. *Kinzua: From Cornplanter to the Corps*, iUniverse, Inc., Lincoln, NE, 2004.

Johnson, Paul E. and Wilentz, Sean. *The Kingdom of Matthias*, Oxford University Press, New York, 1994.

Morrow, Susan Brind. *Wolves and Honey: A Hidden History of the Natural World*, Houghton Mifflin Co., New York, 2004.

Nichols, C. Malcolm. *The Early Post Offices of Chautauqua County, New York*. Jamestown, NY, self published, 1960.

Patterson, Denise Demmer. *Cornplanter Was Here: The Story of a Seneca Chief's Legacy to Oil City*, published by the Oil City Arts Council, Oil City, PA, 2002.

Pettit, Eber M. *Sketches in the History of the Underground Railroad*, "Introduction" and "Notes" by Paul Leone, Region Press, Westfield, NY, 1999.

Priset, W. Duane. "Benjamin Titus Roberts", *American National Bibliography, Vol. 18*, John A. Garranty and Mark C. Carnes, (General Editors), Oxford University Pres, 1999.

Report of the Regents' of the University on the Boundaries Of The State of New York. The Argus Company Printers, New York, 1874.

Robert H. Jackson: Words from His Mighty Pen, Robert H. Jackson Center, Inc., Jamestown, NY.

Spear, John M. *Twenty Years on the Wing: Narrative of Travels and Labors as Missionary Sent Forth by the Association of Beneficents in the Spirit-Land*, W. White and Co., Boston, 1873.

Stonehouse, Helena M. *One Hundred and Forty Years of Methodism in the Jamestown, N. Y. Area*, Parthenon.

Tobin, Jacqueline and Raymond G. Dobbard. *Hidden in Plain View: The Secret Story of Quilts and the Underground Railroad*, Doubleday, New York, 1999.

Twain, Mark. *Life on the Mississippi*. Penguin Books, New York, 1984 (originally published by James R. Osgood, 1883.)

Van Diver, Bradford B. *Roadside Geology of New York*, Mountain Press Publishing Company, Missoula, MT, 1985.

Weisberg, Barbara. *Talking to the Dead: Kate and Maggie Fox and the Rise of Spiritualism*, HarperCollins Publishers, Inc., New York, 2004.

Wicker, Christine. *Lily Dale: The True Story of the Town That Talks to the Dead*, HarperCollins Publishers, Inc., New York, 2004.

Wills, Gary. *Lincoln at Gettysburg: The Words That Remade America*, Simon and Schuster, New York, 1992.

Young, Andrew W. "Kiantone", *History of Chautauqua County, New York, From the First Settlement to the Present Time*, Printing House of Matthew & Warren, Buffalo, NY, 1875.

ARTICLES IN NEWSPAPERS, MAGAZINES, AND OTHER RESOURCES

"A Spiritualist Convention in Chautauqua". *New York Daily Tribune*, September 27, 1858.

Bailey, William S. "Kiantone Mystery Solved as Hidden Cave Is Unearthed", *Jamestown Evening Journal*, November 18, 1933.

Bailey, William S. "The Kiantone Spiritualists and Their River Expedition", *Jamestown Evening Post-Journal*, November 11-12, 1943.

Bailey, William S. "Wealth of Material Dealing with Spiritualist Community at Kiantone is Found in Attic", *Jamestown Post-Journal*, November 26, 1940.

Byrne, Richard M. "Harmonia: Town that Love Built, Killed by Hate, Fear, Suspicion", *The Jamestown Sun*, August 1, 1958.

"Equality Reached in 'Harmonia'". Newspaper source unknown, October 25, 1975.

Finch, Ray. "Fabled Harmonia Lingers in Spirit", *The Jamestown Sun*, September 1, 1949.

"Gerald Staples Retires as City Court Clerk". *Jamestown Post-Journal*, June 28, 1960.

"Gerald Stapes Dies; Ex-Clerk of City Court". *Jamestown Post-Journal*, August 22, 1960.

"Gerald G. Staples, Ex-Clerk of City Court, Dies at Age 70". *Jamestown Post-Journal*, August 22, 1960.

Hand, Jack. "Kiantone Valley Ruins Mark Man's Quest for Perfection", newspaper unknown and the only date available is March 29.

Lindstrom, E. George. "Utopia: The Lost Dream City (The City of Spiritual Springs)", *unnamed Cleveland Ohio newspaper*, April 27, 1938.

"Lingers in Spirit: Indians, Colonists Recognized Kiantone's Mystic Destiny". *Jamestown Sun*, September 1, 1949.

"List of Vessels in Port of New Orleans" and "Steamboat Departures This Day". *New Orleans Daily Crescent*, January 1, 1860 - June 30, 1860.

Priset, Duane W. "Old Jeffrey, The Ghost of Epworth Isle of Axholme, England (Heritage Story)", presentation at the Catch the Spirit Gathering, Niagara Frontier District, Western New York Conference, The United Methodist Church, 2005.

Richards, Joyce. "The State Line In 1788 (Or '92), It Changed", *Jamestown The P-J Weekender*, December 23, 1978.

Sterling, J.M. Letter to the Editor, *The Spiritual Telegraph*, VIII (November 20, 1858), 297.

Streeter, C.S. *Return to Yesterday: A History of Wardsboro, Vermont*, Phoenix Publishing, Canaan, NH, 1980.

Telegraph Papers, IV (February to May, 1854).

"The Spiritual Meeting". *Jamestown Weekly Journal,* September 24, 1858.

"The Spiritual Springs". *Jamestown Weekly Journal,* April 22, 1853.

"The Spiritual Springs Once More". *Jamestown Weekly Journal,* December 23, 1853.

Towery, Jim. "A Mud Patty from the Magic Waters of Kiantone Creek Sparked the Start of the Area's Strangest Religious Colony", *The North East* [PA] *Breeze,* date unknown.

Towery, Jim. "Kiantone's Harmonia Colony Once Built Perpetual Motion Machine But Angry Mob Destroyed It", *The North East* [PA] *Breeze,* date unknown.

Young, John L. "Kiantone Harmonia: Free Love in the 1800's". *Chautauqua Mirror,* September/October 1997.

WEBSITE ARTICLES AND WEBSITE ADDRESSES

It is common today to say that there is a lot of good information and a lot of bad information on the Internet. The websites I used in researching this book appeared to be striving for excellence.

Some of the websites addresses listed below indicate author, article, and website address. Others have just one or two pieces of this information. In a few cases just the subject of the article and the website address are cited.

"African American History of Western New York". The Circle Association, *www.math.buffalo.edu/sww/0history/1830-1865.*

Belote, Thom. "Thomas Jefferson", *www.uua.org.*

Buescher, John. "John Murray Spear", *www.uua.org*.

Buescher, John. "Jesse Babcock Ferguson", *www.uua.org*.

Casara, Ernest. "Hosea Ballou", *www.uua.org*.

"Celtic Indians". *www.newworldcelts.org/celticindians*.

"Choctaw Removal Was Really a 'Trail of Tears'". *www.tc.umn.edu*.

Hilldebrand, Randal. "The Oneida Community", *www.nyhistory. com*.

"George Haskell". *www.cyberdriveillinois.com*.

Howe, Charles A. "Benjamin Rush", *www.uua.org*.

"John Brown". www.wikipedia.org.

Leverton, John. "Wilberforce Colony: Biddulph Township", *http://lucanheritage.tripod.com/history*.

Parker, Peter T. "The Poughkeepsie Seer", *www.anomalist.com*.

"Thaddeus Sheldon". *www.rootsweb.com/~usgenealogy/ny/cattarauqus/bios*.

"The Arian Controversy primer [*sic*]: Pierce and Hallett". *www. bartleby.com*.

"Thomas Clarkson". *www.anti-slaverysociety.org*.

Unitarian Universalist of America Website (History). Several articles came from this website, which provides excellent research materials with an understandable slant towards the various persons with Universalist Unitarian connections. *www.uua.org*.

Wilson, Gregory. "The Abolitionists in and around Sugar Grove Borough, Warren County, PA", *www.madbbs.com/users/sgrove/ AreaAbolitionists*.

"William Wilberforce (1759-1833)". *www.britannia.com/bios*.

www.spirithistory.com. This site includes the references to *The Spiritual Telegraph* as well as the various lists of Spiritualists that were compiled during the 1850s and 1860s and reports about Spiritualist conventions. This is a very helpful website for such details.

"Zaccheus Hamblin". *http://home.earthlink.net/~anderson207/Hamblen.htm*.

OTHER SOURCES

Bailey, William S. "The Kiantone Valley and the Association of Beneficients", paper read before the meeting of the Jamestown University Club at Kiantone, N.Y., June 27, 1924.

Connelly, Mary. "Kiantone to Frewsburg, Harmonia to Oakknoll: The Cults," unpublished academic term paper, 1986.

Duino, Russell. *The Domain at Spiritual Springs: A Short History of the Kiantone Harmonia, Together with a Calendar of the Sheldon Papers from the Collection of Ernest C. Miller, Warren, Pennsylvania*, unpublished Masters Thesis, Western Reserve University, June, 1959.

Forsberg, Grace. "The William Storum Family: About the Facts and Incidences Pertaining to One of the Three Most Prominent Abolitionist Families in the Town of Busti", unpublished.

Greaves, Dr. James P. Letter written to Dr. J.F. Gray, January 24, 1853, published in the 1853 *Spiritual Telegraph* and appears in other resources, including Hardinge's history of American Spiritualism.

Interview, Deborah K. Cronin with Norman P. Carlson. Busti, NY, April 22, 2005.

Interview, E.C. Miller with John M. Cushman, Jeweler. Jamestown, N.Y. January 21, 1949.

Interview, Ernest C. Miller with Mrs. Margaret Fish. Randolph, N.Y., June 5, 1947.

Jackson, Robert H. Letter (photocopy at Myers Memorial Library, Frewsburg, NY), to Ruth Sternberg, July 7, 1951.

Patriot Colony documents. Switzerland County Library, Vevay, IN, unpublished.

"We Salute The Town of Kiantone", One page description of Town of Kiantone. source unknown.

Yaw, Gregory. "An American Worldview: The Cosmos and Society in a Radical Milieu on the Eve of the Civil War", Bachelor of Arts with Honors Paper, Unpublished, Amherst College, MA, 1972.

[1]   Cronin, Deborah K., *Holy Ground: Celtic Christian Spirituality,* Upper Room Books, Nashville, TN, 1999, p. 120.

[2] Hoover, N. William, *Kinzua: From Cornplanter to the Corp,* iUniverse, Inc., Lincoln, NE, 2004, p. 7.

[3] Clarke, Maj. E. W., *Reports of the Regents' Boundary Commission upon the New York and Pennsylvania Border,* Weed, Parsons and Company, 1886, foldout map inserted in book cover.

[4] It is a bit of a challenge to locate precisely the *Outlet, The Rapids,* and the *Chadakoin River,* since this connected chain of water features begins with the Outlet at the end of the lake, today's village of *Celeron,* but then moves into The Rapids near Jamestown's electric plant and then becomes the Chadakoin River. It is, I think, a matter of degree and water activity without strict boundaries. Today, someone with a GPS Locator could have some fun attempting to record the exact locations.

[5] It is commonly understood in the Jamestown area that this *is the only place where a river (the Chadakoin) flows into a creek (the Conewango),* but I do not know if that claim has been extensively researched and proven.

[6] The use of the verb "were" is used here since at that time many of its states considered the United States to be a loosely united group of separate state entities. The country only became *the* United States, as in one strongly united country, following the Civil War. Obviously, not all Americans shared the notion that pre-Civil War United States was one indivisible country, a situation that led to the war itself.

[7] Genealogy material in this chapter was provided by Karen Livsey, librarian and genealogist, who is associated with the Fenton

History Center – Museum and Library. Mrs. Livsey's source for this information is, *Return to Yesterday: A History of Wardsboro, Vermont,* by C.S. Streeter, Phoenix Publishing, Camden, NH, 1980.

[8] Pettit, Eber M. *Sketches of the History of the Underground Railroad,* complete with Introduction and Notes by Paul Leone, was published in 1999 by Chautauqua Region Press and is available through the Fenton History Center-Museum and Library in Jamestown.

[9] Much of the preceding material comes from "African American History of Western New York State 1830-1865", located at www.math. buffalo.edu/~ww/0history/1830-1865. It is an excellent source of information with much more detail than noted here.

[10] Priset, Duane W., "A History of the Western New York Conference," unpublished article, p.5.

[11] Cross, Whitney R., *The Burned-over District: The Social and Intellectual History of Enthusiastic Religions in Western New York, 1800-1850,* Ithaca and London, Cornell University Press, 1950, p. 3.

[12] *Upstate New York*, by my definition, is everything north and west of Yonkers, a town located a few miles above New York City. *Western New York*, again by my definition, is everything west of a line drawn from Lake Ontario just east of Rochester down to the Pennsylvania state line. All New Yorkers are not alike. There are vast regional, economic, and sociological differences among the peoples of this state.

[13] Hillebrand, Randall, "The Oneida Community", *www.nyhistory.com*.

[14] Park, Peter T. "The Poughkeepsie Seer", *www.anomalist.com*.

[15] Cronin, p. 34.

[16] Cronin, p. 33.

[17] Spear, John Murray, *Twenty Years on The Wing: Brief Narrative of My Travels and Labors as a Missionary Sent Forth and Sustained by the Association of Beneficents in Spirit Land,* William White and Company, Boston, 1873, p. 11.

[18] Spear, p. 9.

[19] The term, "Dowie-like," referring to how Spear caught fish, occurs in several secondary sources, but the primary source for this bit

of information is found in Oliver F. Chase's article, "The Kiantone Movement", *Centennial History of Chautauqua County,* Chautauqua History Co., Jamestown, NY, 1904, II, 826-830. I had no idea what it meant, and neither did any of my fishing friends. After a lengthy search at the library, various bookstores, and the Internet, I came to the conclusion that it is a shortened version of the fishing term, *downrigger.* This style of fishing, popular on the Great Lakes and other fresh water fishing sites, uses two lines, one a heavily weighted line attached to the boat by a winch and a second line and lure, attached both to the end of the fishing pole and the weighted line so to be held at the proper fishing depth. When the fish takes the lure, the fishing rod line is released from the weighed line via a special clip. Chase notes that he has a somewhat hazy recollection of Spear fishing in this manner "at the old Prendergast dam near the Springs", p. 828.

[20] The website, *www.uua.org,* is an excellent source for the history and theology of this denomination.

[21] Casara, Ernest, "Hosea Ballou", *www.uua.org.*

[22] Buescher, John, "John Murray Spear", *www.uua.org.*

[23] Spear, p. 13.

[24] Spear, p. 13.

[25] Spear, p. 15.

[26] An educated guess is that by "Franklin" was meant "Benjamin Franklin". His first name alone would have sufficed within the context of this list of persons.

[27] Spear, pp. 16-17.

[28] Spear, p. 17.

[29] Spear, pp. 18 and 20.

[30] Spear, p. 19.

[31] Spear, p. 21.

[32] Spear, p. 21.

[33] Spear, p. 22.

[34] Spear, p. 22.

[35]*Sheldon Papers*, Darlington Memorial Collection, University of Pittsburgh, Doc. No. 1.

[36] Spear, p. 22.

[37] Spear, p. 22.

[38] Spear, p. 23.

[39] Spear, p. 27.

[40] Spear, pp. 23-25.

[41] Spear, p. 26.

[42] Spear, p. 26.

[43] Spear, p. 26.

[44] I found his name, together with the clergy title, in an article, "1854 New England Spiritualists' Association", *www.spirithistory.com*.

[45] "*Spiritual Telegraph*, (New York, May 27 and June 24)", *www.spirithistory.com*.

[46]*www.rootsweb.com/~usgenweb/ny/cattaraugus/bios*.

[47] *Sheldon Papers*, Doc. No. 62.

[48]*www.cyberdriveillinois.com*.

[49] "*The Spiritual Telegraph*, New York, August 23 and September 6", *www.spirithistory.com*.

[50] Howe, Charles A., "Benjamin Rush", *www.uua.org*.

[51] Thom Belote, "Thomas Jefferson", *www.uua.org*.

[52] Again, as stated in Chapter 6, no first name is mentioned, although it does appear when Franklin is listed with the Association of Beneficients.

[53] Information about Zaccheus Hamblin is located on a family genealogy site, *http://home.earthlink.net/~anderson207/Hamblen.htm*.

[54] Again, thanks to Karen Livsey for digging out this genealogical tidbit!

[55]"The Arian Controversy primer [*sic*]: Pierce and Hallett", *www.bartleby.com*.

[56] Material about Thomas Clarkson is found at *www.anti-slaverysociety*. Sadly, slavery still exists today, necessitating the on-going work of

this group.

57 *Sheldon Papers*.Doc. No. 1.

* I use the terms, "Harmonia" and "Domain" interchangeably in this book, as well as simply referring to the Spiritualist community that existed during the 1850's and 1860's as "Kiantone." There are times when "Kiantone" also refers to the actual hamlet and its residents. The reader should be able to sort these usages out by context.

58 *Sheldon Papers*, Doc. No. 1.

59 Spear, p. 22.

60 Spear, p. 22.

61 Spear, p. 27.

62 Spear, p. 27.

63 Genealogical information, again, courtesy of Karen Livsey.

64 Chase, p. 829.

65 Spear, p. 27.

66 Spear, p. 27.

67 Spear, p. 27-28

68 "Spiritual Telegraph (August 23 and September 6, 1856)", *www. spirithistory.com*.

69 Spear's pamphlet was published in 1873, although he may have written it in 1872.

70 Chase, p. 829.

71 Chase, p. 829. Oliver F. Chase suggests that it was John Chase's sons who did the digging. This is likely, since Chase was just a youth then, too. No doubt the boys commiserated together about the hard work they were doing.

72 Hardinge, Emma, *Modern American Spiritualism: A Twenty Years' Record of the Communion Between Earth and the World of Spirits*, University Books, New Hyde Park, New York, 1970 (originally published in 1869), p. 232.

73 Greaves, Dr. James P., letter written to Dr. J. F. Gray, January 24, 1853. It was published in the 1853 *Spiritual Telegraph*, and appears in other

resources, including Hardinge's history of American Spiritualism.

[74] Greaves' letter.

[75] "A Spiritualist Convention in Chautauqua: A Harmonial City to Be Founded", *New York Daily Tribune*, September 21, 1858.

[76] *New York Daily Tribune*, September 21, 1858.

[77] Spear, p. 22.

[78] *Sheldon Papers*, Doc. No. 53. In this document Spear writes to Sheldon saying that he is going to Niagara Falls with Caroline Hinckley. It seems possible that if Spear was going to Niagara Falls that he either was already in Kiantone or planning to visit there soon.

[79] Cheney, Mark, interview by William S. Bailey, 1924, appears in various resources.

[80] *Jamestown Journal*, April 22, 1853.

[81] Chase, p. 829.

[82] Chase, p. 830.

[83] Chase, p. 830.

[84] Chase, p. 829.

[85] Chase, p. 828.

[86] *New York Daily Tribune*, September 21, 1858.

[87] Yaw, Gregory, citing *The Educator*, pp. 342-343, 346-350, 387, 390, appearing as p. 180-181, in Yaw's paper, "An American Worldview: Cosmos and Society in a Radical Worldview on the Eve of the Civil War", Bachelor of Arts with Honors Paper, Unpublished, Amherst College, MA, 1972.

[88] This information was found at *www.tulane.edu/~/Greeley*. Alas, with the devastation *Hurricane Katrina* wrecked upon this university, they were unable to provide me with a clearer reference notation.

[89] Chase, p. 829.

[90] Hardinge, 234.

[91] Cheney interview.

[92] Spear, p. 21.

[93] "Massachusetts Spiritual Convention", *www.spirithistory.com*.

[94] "Call for a National Spiritualist Convention", *www.spirithistory.com*.

[95] Crocker, Kathleen and Currie, Jane. *Images of America – Jamestown*, Arcadia Publishing, Portsmouth, NH, 2004, p. 23. They could only have come part-way by train, as the first train line, the *Atlantic and Great Western Railroad*, did not arrive in Jamestown until August 25, 1860, almost a year later.

[96] The *Erie Canal*, as the song states, stretched across New York State "from Albany to Buffalo". The *Genesee Canal*, a short-lived venture, ran from Rochester to just east of Olean, NY.

[97] *www.spirithistory.com*.

[98] *New York Daily Tribune*, September 21, 1858.

[99] *New York Daily Tribune*, September 21, 1858.

[100] *New York Daily Tribune*, September 21, 1858.

[101] *Jamestown Weekly Journal*, September 24, 1858.

[102] *Jamestown Weekly Journal*, September 24, 1858.

[103] *New York Daily Tribune*, September 21, 1858.

[104] *New York Daily Tribune*, September 21, 1858.

[105] "Fourth Annual Spiritual Register", *www.spirithistory.com*.

[106] *New York Daily Tribune*, September 21, 1858.

[107] *New York Daily Tribune*, September 21, 1858.

[108] *New York Daily Tribune*, September 21, 1858.

[109] *Jamestown Weekly Journal*, September 24, 1858.

[110] *Jamestown Weekly Journal*, September 24, 1858.

[111] *Jamestown Weekly Journal*, September 24, 1858.

[112] *Jamestown Weekly Journal*, September, 24, 1858.

[113] *Spiritual Telegraph*, p. 297, November 20, 1858.

[114] *Spiritual Telegraph*, November 20, 1858.

[115] "Movements of Spiritualists". *New York Daily Times*, October 14, 1858, as quoted by Gregory Yaw in his academic paper, pp. 196-197.

[116] Yaw, pp. 197-199 [*sic*, p. 198 is a photo].

[117] *Sheldon Papers*, Doc. No. 14.

[118] *www.wikipedia.org.*

[119] *Sheldon Papers*, Doc. No. 28.

[120] *www.tc.umn.edu.*

[121] *Sheldon Papers*, Doc. No. 31.

[122] *Sheldon Papers*, Doc. No. 35.

[123] Document found in Switzerland County Public Library, Vevay, IN.

[124] *Sheldon Papers*, Doc. No. 46.

[125] *Sheldon Papers*, Doc. No. 49.

[126] *Sheldon Papers*, Doc. No. 59.

[127] *Sheldon Papers*, Doc. No. 60.

[128] *Sheldon Papers*, Doc. No. 61.

[129] *Sheldon Papers*, Doc. No. 62.

[130] *Sheldon Papers*, Doc. No. 58.

[131] *Sheldon Papers*, Doc. No. 115. ·

[132] *Sheldon Papers*, Doc. No. 117.

[133] Hardinge, p. 237.

[134] Hardinge, p. 238.

[135] Hardinge, p. 234.

[136] Edson, Obed, *History of Chautauqua County, N. Y.*, Boston, W.A. Ferguson and Co., 1984.

[137] Hardinge, p. 238.

[138] *Sheldon Papers*, Doc. No. 53.

[139] *Sheldon Papers*, Doc. No. 52.

[140] *Sheldon Papers*, Doc. No. 131.

[141] *SheldonPapers*, Doc. No. 134.

[142] *Sheldon Papers*, Doc. No. 269.

[143] *Sheldon Papers*, Doc. No. 255.

[144] *Sheldon Papers*, Doc. No. 263.

[145] *Sheldon Papers*, Doc. No. 252.

[146] "1864 Progressive Annual", *www.spirithistory.org*.

[147] *Sheldon Papers*, Doc. No. 93.

[148] *Sheldon Papers*, Doc. No. 198.

[149] *Sheldon Papers*, Doc. No. 67, 98, 99, 121, 122.

[150] Spear, p. 37.

[151] *Sheldon Papers*, Doc. No. 154.

[152] Buescher, John, "Jesse Babcock Ferguson", *www.uua.org*.

[153] Clark, p. 91.

[154] Clark, p. 91.

[155] All letters referred to in this section are housed with the *Sheldon Papers* in Pittsburgh, but they are not numbered documents nor is there a catalogue card for them.

[156] *Robert H. Jackson: Words from His Mighty Pen*, Robert H. Jackson Center, Inc., Jamestown, NY.

[157] Jackson, Robert H., letter to Miss Ruth Sternberg, written on *Supreme Court of the United States* stationary, photocopy available at the Myers Memorial Library, Frewsburg, NY, July 7, 1951.

Printed in the United States
145312LV00001B/91/A

9 781425 934750